DEEP-WATER

TELEOSTEAN FISHES

OF CALIFORNIA

BY

JOHN E. FITCH

AND

ROBERT J. LAVENBERG

UNIVERSITY OF CALIFORNIA PRESS

BERKELEY AND LOS ANGELES: 1968

UNIVERSITY OF CALIFORNIA PRESS

BERKELEY AND LOS ANGELES, CALIFORNIA

CAMBRIDGE UNIVERSITY PRESS

LONDON, ENGLAND

LIBRARY OF CONGRESS CATALOG CARD NUMBER: 68-64172

PRINTED IN THE UNITED STATES OF AMERICA

CONTENTS

Illustration on cover: Opah, *Lampris regius*

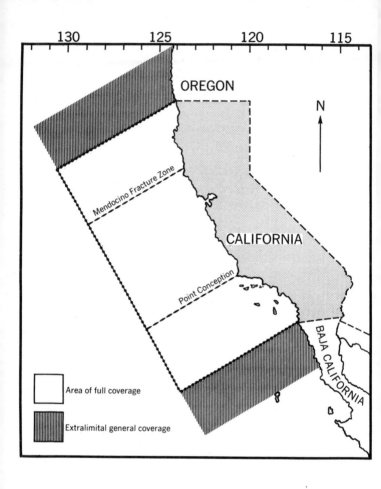

Area of Coverage for California Deep-Water Fishes.

INTRODUCTION

If all the fishes in the world's oceans could be accurately counted, we feel certain that the individuals belonging to two families of deep-sea fishes (Myctophidae and Gonostomatidae) would contribute about half of the final tally. Before anyone decides to rush out and catch this untapped resource to start feeding the world's protein-starved multitudes, we would like to point out that, even though a few kinds of lanternfishes might weigh four ounces each, a dozen other kinds never exceed a quarter of an ounce each when full-grown, and a million bristlemouths would not keep a kitten in food for more than a week. Add to this the fact that even with today's finest midwater trawls, with sonar devices that can locate zones of greatest fish concentration (deep-scattering layers), and with electronic gear to inform shipboard personnel when the net has reached the exact depth of a scattering layer, a two- to five-hour tow rarely yields more than twenty pounds of bathypelagic fishes.

We believe that at present the greatest value of the myriads of mesopelagic and bathypelagic fishes is in providing forage for predatory species, some of which (e.g., tunas, swordfishes, salmons) are heavily exploited by man. However, some of our colleagues feel that the greatest potential of these fishes is to satisfy man's intellectual curiosity regarding the functional significance of their diversified bizarre adaptations. Despite such differences, we must continue to send scientific expeditions to explore the depths of the sea and to study the interrelationships of the creatures we capture. Such action should satisfy the research needs of academicians, and is the only way that we can hope to obtain enough information to manage these resources wisely should their harvest become essential to an overpopulated, protein-starved world.

Reliable estimates indicate that there are between 15,000 and 17,000 kinds of fishes living in the world today. Possibly half of these are freshwater and estuarine species, and half are marine. California's marine fish fauna comprises at least 525 species of bony fishes belonging to about 160 families. Our listing of deepwater fishes (p. 138) includes just under 260 species (48 percent of the state's total) belonging to 71 families (44 percent of the total), and additional species are being captured each year. However, not all the fishes we have listed can be considered true mesopelagic, bathypelagic, or abyssal species.

The largest deep-sea fish recorded from California was a 22-foot oarfish weighing an estimated 500 pounds that stranded itself near Newport Beach in 1901. The louvar, at 7 feet and 300 pounds, is probably the second largest; ribbonfishes, lancetfishes, and a few others might approach the louvar in length, but only the opah can compete with it in weight. Our smallest species is probably the topside lampfish, *Notolychnus valdiviae*, which when full grown rarely exceeds an inch in length. Few of the sixteen species of lightfishes (family Gonostomatidae) exceed 3 inches when full-grown, and some never attain 2 inches.

SCOPE OF COVERAGE

We have attempted to mention all bathypelagic and bottom-living species that have been reported from within three natural faunal zones (i.e., our northern, central, and southern subregions), and offshore to the approximate outer limit of the California Current. Our northern subregion extends southward from the boundary of the ridge and trough province of the eastern north Pacific (approximate latitude 43° N.) to the Mendocino fracture zone (approximate latitude 40° N.). Our central subregion includes most of the state's offshore waters between the Mendocino fracture zone and Point Conception, and our southern subregion takes in waters as far south as Guadalupe Island, an area which receives recruitment from subtropical waters even farther south. Thus our general area of coverage extends from about 100 miles north of California to about 200 miles south of California, and offshore some 350 to 400 miles. Fishes which are known only from south or north of California's borders or from well offshore have not been included in our species list (p. 138), but we have mentioned them in our general accounts.

The selection of deep-water fishes or fish families is entirely of our choosing, and we assume full responsibility for the species included as well as any omissions that may have occurred. In some species (e.g., cusk-eels, poachers, and snake-eels) the adults are seldom found a great distance offshore or at great depth, but the larvae and early juveniles are commonly caught with midwater trawling gear over extremely deep water. For these, perhaps we should have illustrated larvae or young stages, but we chose to show the adults. In other species (e.g., snailfishes, eelpouts, and brotulas) some family members always inhabit abyssal depths, but others live within a stone's throw of shore. For these families we have listed all species, but only the deepwater forms have been discussed in detail.

We have not included several kinds of fishes commonly taken as larvae in midwater trawls (e.g., long-spined channel rockfish and various sanddabs) or captured only as bottom-dwelling adults in very deep water (e.g., flabby sculpin and deep-sea sole) because it seems more appropriate to consider their families in future booklets dealing with food and game fishes and tidepool fishes.

We have illustrated a "typical" member of each family, and have attempted to explain how this one species can be distinguished from all others in our waters. Natural history notes are as complete as our information on the subject, but since few life-history studies have been conducted on deep-sea fishes, we often found it necessary to examine otoliths and scales for evidence of age, to check stomachs to learn of feeding habits, and to inspect sections of ovaries under the microscope to detect signs of maturity. We have presented fishery information, sofar as is known, for the species discussed, and have listed other family members in our general accounts. We have not included keys for identifying other family members, but if these are not abundant we have, in narrative style, given information for distinguishing them. For some of the larger families (i.e., Gonostomatidae, Myctophidae, Melamphaidae, Liparididae, Agonidae, Zoarcidae), technical publications are available, although not always up to date, to aid in identification, and we have included references to these in our list of suggested reading.

All the illustrations were drawn or reconstructed from freshly preserved specimens or, for large unwieldy species, from photographs of freshly caught fishes. We did not feel it was necessary to outline scales on all species which have them.

Our systematic arrangement of families is according to generally accepted usage, with slight modification based upon a recently proposed classification.

SPECIAL ADAPTATIONS OF SOME DEEP-WATER FISHES

The deep-sea environment creates many problems for the fishes inhabiting it that their shallower-living relatives do not encounter. Three factors that probably have the greatest influence upon the lives of the creatures living at these depths are the failure of solar light to penetrate very far beneath the surface, the lack of seasonal change (a constant temperature of about 4° C), and the absence of primary organic productivity. Because of these adversities, or in spite of them, many deep-living fishes have developed special structures, functions, and behavioral patterns which increase their chances of survival both as individuals and as species.

Since survival basically depends upon success in feeding and reproduction, most adaptations, modifications, or specializations appear to be designed to assist in carrying out these two functions. Food-gathering adaptations include angling devices, distensible stomachs, large mouths, formidable jaw teeth for catching and holding prey, visual acuity, and so on. Reproductive success may be enhanced by development of photophores which aid in mate recognition, by the tendency toward functional hermaphroditism among many groups, by the presence of parasitic males, and by other equally helpful (to the fishes) but less spectacular (to us) specializations.

Luminescing organs (photophores) are widespread among fishes inhabiting depths where light fails to penetrate. In a nine-year study of an area south of Bermuda just eight miles in diameter, 1,500 hauls with a fine-mesh net at depths of 400 to 1,400 fathoms yielded over 115,000 fishes representing 46 families, 65 genera, and 220 species. Luminosity was present in 39 percent of the families, 81 percent of the genera, 66 percent of the species, and 96 percent of the individuals. In 1966 Robert J. Lavenberg conducted a similar study during a research cruise from New Zealand to Chile along the Subtropic Convergence. During this cruise, 20,479 bathypelagic fishes, caught with a midwater trawl, represented 34 families, 79 genera, and 154 species. Two of the families contained some genera that had luminescing organs and other genera that did not, but at generic and specific levels luminous organs either were present or were absent. An analysis, similar to the Bermuda study, showed luminosity in 39 percent of the families, 59 percent of the genera, 67 percent of the species, and 98 percent of the individuals.

An angling device or lure may be a modified dorsal-fin spine on the head, as in the anglerfishes, or it may be the "chin whisker," or mental barbel, sported by scaleless dragonfishes and their relatives. Stargazers are known to bury themselves in the bottom and twitch their eyes to attract small shrimp, crabs, and fishes. When these approach the stargazer's bait, its large horizontally positioned mouth is a perfect trap. The elongate gulpers, with a luminous lure near the tip of the tail, would need to swim in circles for the device to be useful.

Many of our midwater fishes have very large eyes (e.g., mirror dory, oxeye oreo, oarfish, crestfish) which presumably are helpful in gathering what little light there is at the depths they inhabit. The telescopic eyes of the barreleye, *Macropinna*, and some of its relatives, hatchetfishes of the genus *Argyropelecus*, and the telescopefish, *Bathyleptus*, are more difficult to explain, especially since in some of these the eyes point straight up. Recently it was found that the barreleye and its family relatives (Opisthoproctidae) have two pairs of eyes — a large pair of telescopic eyes believed to function as light-gatherers, and a small eye at the base of each large eye which probably focuses the image gathered by the large eye. Prior to this discovery the small eye was thought to be an orbital photophore.

The fishes with extremely large mouths, noted for swallowing their prey whole, include gulpers, whalefishes, anglerfishes, the lancetfish, and the loosejaw. Among these the anglerfishes are very toothy, as is the lancetfish, but the viperfish, daggertooth, and needletooth swallower, to name a few, are even more toothy. Among those with the most distensible stomachs are swallowers, gulpers, anglerfishes, dragonfishes, and the lancetfish.

In several families of anglerfishes the males (very tiny) are parasitic on the females (very large). Once the male is attached to the body of the female it loses all resemblance to a fish as we know it, and becomes little more than a living sperm packet. Some deep-sea fishes have apparently solved the problem of locating a mate by becoming hermaphrodites (e.g., lancetfishes and barracudinas), perhaps being capable of self-fertilization. As other species are studied, this phenomenon may be found to be more prevalent than current knowledge indicates.

The color of most bathypelagic and abyssal fishes is dark black or brownish black, and a few species are red (the first color spectrum filtered out by seawater; so red appears black at relatively shallow depths). The fishes believed to inhabit shallower depths than the bathypelagics (known as mesopelagic fishes) often have silver-colored bodies and crimson fins. Off our coast, these include the opah, louvar, oarfish, crestfish, and ribbonfishes.

Deep-sea fishes show numerous other modifications. Most of them have poorly ossified, lightweight skeletons (apparently helpful in maintaining buoyancy with a minimum of effort); many species are scaleless (possibly of hydrodynamic importance); many have elongate "streaming" bodies or fins, and often parts of these are missing as if grabbed by a predator, so this trait may be useful in survival; many larvae are transparent and live in shallower environments (apparently assuring a full stomach and some protection against predators); larval forms may be stalk-eyed as well as transparent(possibly helpful in flotation or mimicry); and some predatory species have black-lined stomachs — possibly to keep the luminous fish which they swallow whole from "lighting up" in their death struggles and making the predator an easy meal for a larger fish. The functions of most of these modifications are not yet clearly understood, but increased use of underwater research vehicles should eventually enable us to explain them.

A Brief History of Deep-Water Ichthyology Affecting California

Bathypelagic ichthyology began with the *Challenger* expedition during the period 1873-1876; the extensive fish collections from that expedition were described by Albert Günther in 1887. Although the *Challenger* did not work off California, many of the fishes collected during its cruise are known to range throughout the world, including off our shores, and several of the scientific names of our deep-water fishes still bear Dr. Günther's name as describer. Other world expeditions that have made important contributions to the knowledge of our deep-sea fishes, and the ichthyologists who worked on and described the fishes collected by them, were *Travailleur* and *Talisman*, 1880-1883 (Leon L. Vaillant); early collections of the *Blake, Albatross,* and *Fish Hawk* (George B. Goode and Tarleton H. Bean); the Indian survey ship *Investigator* (A. Alcock); and the *Valdivia* expedition of 1898-1899 (A. Brauer).

The U. S. Fish Commission's deep-sea investigations with the steamer *Albatross* in 1888 were the first off California. Fishes collected during this and later trips into the eastern Pacific and off California (1896, 1897, and 1904) were described by Charles H. Gilbert, Alexander Agassiz, and Samuel Garman.

Although in 1854 William O. Ayres described one of the brotulas (*Brosmophycis marginata*) that we have included in this booklet, and Charles F. Girard published accounts of several other species (e.g., *Za-*

niolepis latipinnis and *Otophidium taylori*) in 1857 and 1858, the first truly bathypelagic species were not described until 1880. In that year David Starr Jordan and Charles H. Gilbert published accounts of the myctophid *Tarletonbeania crenularis*, the barracudina *Lestidium ringens*, and the medusafish *Icichthys lockingtoni*, and W. N. Lockington described the ragfish *Icosteus aenigmaticus*. The barracudina described by Jordan and Gilbert was found in the stomach of a Pacific hake which had been taken from the stomach of an albacore. Several other bathypelagic fishes from California, especially lanternfishes, were found in fish stomachs and described by Carl H. Eigenmann and his wife Rosa in 1889 and 1890.

Every decade since has yielded additional new-to-science fish species from off our shores. The most recently described bathypelagics, *Normichthys campbelli* and *Nansenia crassa* were recorded in 1965 by Robert J. Lavenberg.

During the last two decades, numerous research expeditions have been fielded off California (and to other seas) by the U. S. Bureau of Commercial Fisheries, the Scripps Institution of Oceanography, the Allan Hancock Foundation (University of Southern California), and the California Department of Fish and Game. Most bathypelagics collected during these research cruises have been studied by scientists from the various institutions concerned.

CALIFORNIA'S FOSSIL RECORD OF DEEP-WATER FISHES

California is blessed with a rich assemblage of fossil deposits containing fish remains. Skeletal parts and fragments such as teeth, scales, otoliths, vertebrae, fin spines, and miscellaneous other bones, are most numerous, but some fishes were preserved entire, usually as flattened impressions, or even in three-dimensional form.

All types of identifiable fish material abound in deposits of Miocene, Pliocene, and Pleistocene age; scales, otoliths, and teeth are plentiful in Oligocene and Eocene deposits; and recognizable items have been reported from Cretaceous outcrops 125 million or more years old.

Remains of deep-sea fishes are best known from Miocene diatomites and shales, where their intact skeletons form dark "imprints" on a light background. Diatomite quarries at Lompoc have probably yielded the greatest numbers and kinds of beautifully preserved specimens, but Miocene diatomites and shales at or near San Clemente, San Pedro, Walteria, Santa Monica, Pomona, Point Conception, and Taft have produced equally fine material. Many of the fossilized deep-sea fishes in these deposits have retained their luminescent organs (photophores) throughout the 20 to 40 million years they have been interred, and some of these fishes are apparently the same as species that are living off our coast today.

Otoliths (ear stones) of deep-sea fishes, primarily lanternfishes (Myctophidae) have been found in many Miocene deposits east of Bakersfield, and in most southern California marine Pliocene and Pleistocene outcrops. In a Lomita Marl deposit (Pliocene) near San Pedro, several thousand lanternfish otoliths representing fourteen species were recovered from a few hundred pounds of fossil-bearing matrix. Otoliths of deep-sea smelts (Bathylagidae), bigscales (Melamphaidae), rattails (Macrouridae), and codlings (Moridae) were also abundant in this deposit.

Most fish remains found in Miocene and older deposits appear to represent extinct species, but all the otoliths from our Pliocene and Pleistocene are from species that are still alive today.

The Los Angeles County Museum of Natural History contains the largest collection of fossil fishes and fish remains, but an excellent assortment reposes at

Stanford University (Natural History Museum). Numerous small museums, such as the Cabrillo Beach Marine Museum, routinely display fossil fishes common to their area, and have other material on exhibit or in storage, but vast quantities of shark teeth, fish "imprints," and similar items have been found and retained by private individuals. Some of these amateur collectors have done an excellent job of labeling and classifying material in their possession, but most such finds are saved only as curios or oddities, and after gathering dust for years are discarded as junk.

ACKNOWLEDGMENTS

This booklet did not result solely from our own labors; we received help and encouragement from many individuals. To all those who contributed their talents or shared their special knowledge we wish to express our gratitude.

We are especially grateful to the Sport Fishing Institute, Washington, D. C., for financial support which permitted us to obtain illustrations of high quality.

Many of the fishes we examined were collected by personnel working under the guidance of Jay M. Savage, University of Southern California, during research cruises of the *Velero IV* off southern California. Dr. Savage's investigations on the ecology of our offshore basins were supported by several grants from the National Science Foundation, as was the work of John E. Fitch on fish otoliths. Obviously, our coverage could not have been nearly as complete if it had not been for the financial assistance rendered by the National Science Foundation to West Coast research and researchers.

Wayne J. Baldwin, of Honolulu, and Mrs. Evie Templeton, of Los Angeles, produced the superb coquille-board fish portraits.

Invaluable help was obtained from a dozen or more biologists, ichthyologists, scientists, and other specialists. In alphabetical order these are: Shelton Applegate, Los Angeles County Museum, fossil fishes; William L. Craig, California Department of Fish and Game, Terminal Island, *Gempylus* from California; Mike Eckhardt, University of Southern California, hatchetfishes; W. I. Follett, California Academy of Sciences, San Francisco, an unreported brotulid and manuscript review; Paul A. Gregory, California Department of Fish and Game, Menlo Park, mirror dories; Richard Grinols, U. S. Bureau of Commercial Fisheries, Seattle, record sizes of benthic fishes; Richard Haedrich, Museum of Comparative Zoology, Harvard, flotsamfishes; Carl L. Hubbs, Scripps Institution of Oceanography, common names and manuscript review; Shelly Johnson, University of Southern California, eelpouts; George S. Myers, Stanford University, specimen loan; Basil Nafpaktitis, University of Southern California, lanternfishes; John Paxton, University of Southern California, lanternfishes and whalefishes; C. Richard Robins, University of Miami, cusk-eels; Richard Rosenblatt, Scripps Institution of Oceanography, eels, specimen loan, and manuscript review; Boyd W. Walker, University of California, Los Angeles, specimen loans; and Vladimir Walters, University of California, Los Angeles, loan of an oarfish picture.

Loretta M. Morris, of San Pedro, and Betty Ponti and Dorothy Fink, of Los Angeles, typed the manuscript drafts; and Arline Fitch was always available to read proof or to listen to various sections being read aloud to see if they "sounded satisfactory."

ALEPOCEPHALIDAE (SLICKHEAD FAMILY)
California Slickhead
Alepocephalus tenebrosus Gilbert

Distinguishing characters. — The uniformly dark dull brown coloration and the soft mushy texture of the flesh tend to separate the California slickhead from all other midwater forms. Small cycloid (smooth) scales cover the entire body, but are absent on the head, typical of the alepocephalids. The texture of the integument on the head is smooth and thin. Additional features are the posteriorly placed and subequal median fins, the weakly ossified jaws with poorly developed dentition, and an upper jaw that extends no farther backward than the anterior margin of the eye.

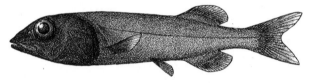

Fig. 1. *Alepocephalus tenebrosus*

Natural history notes. — *Alepocephalus tenebrosus* is taken relatively infrequently in midwater trawling operations off California. Adults are taken in deep hauls near the bottom, but, since none of the species that occur off California migrates into shallow oceanic zones at night, it is assumed that slickheads live in close association with the bottom. "Free-vehicle" set lines utilized in very deep water by personnel of the Scripps Institution of Oceanography capture fair numbers of large specimens of *A. tenebrosus* on the bottom. However, half-grown and juvenile individuals live in the midwaters well above the bottom. Slickheads are seldom captured in waters shallower than 1,500 feet, but range from 150 feet (sometimes) into depths exceeding 18,000 feet.

Alepocephalus tenebrosus has a limited distribution in the eastern parts of the Pacific Ocean. Few members of the family are found in all oceans; most of them are restricted to limited regions. Specimens attain a length of 2 feet or more and a weight of slightly less than three pounds. The otoliths from a 15-inch fish had three winter rings; so a 2-footer might be ten or more years old if one allows for slowing of growth with age. Slickheads would certainly be regarded as inferior food because of their soft, fleshy texture. Most members of the family apparently feed on small crustaceans. The soft jaws typical of the family would hardly be capable of holding large prey. To our knowledge, alepocephalids do not serve as food for any larger carnivore of the sea.

Fishery information. — Slickheads have been taken by a number of methods including deep set lines, scientific midwater trawling gear, commercial otter trawls, and fine-meshed plankton nets. A large specimen was taken off Eureka, California, in 25 fathoms.

Other family members. — The most recent taxonomic revision recognizes twenty-four genera. Seven genera (and species) are known to occur off California: *Photostylus*, in which the head and body are covered with scattered photophores on stalks; *Bajacalifornia* and *Narcetes*, both having an advanced dorsal fin, with *Bajacalifornia* distinguished by the prominent ventral knob on the lower jaw; *Ericara*, with an anal fin in advance of the dorsal fin; *Talismania*, with a prolonged first pectoral fin ray; and *Brunichthys* and *Alepocephalus*, much like *Talismania* but lacking prolonged pectoral fin rays. *Brunichthys* can be distinguished from *Alepocephalus* by having only one supramaxillary instead of two.

Meaning of name.—*Alepocephalus* (head without scales) *tenebrosus* (dark or gloomy, coming from the great depths where not even shadows occur).

SEARSIIDAE (TUBESHOULDER FAMILY)
Shining Tubeshoulder
Sagamichthys abei Parr

Distinguishing characters. — Tubeshoulders are easily distinguished from all other fishes by the tube-like projection pointing posteriorly just above the pectoral fin. The shining tubeshoulder is covered with small cycloid scales, and in the region of the shoulder tube the attachment of each scale changes from the anterior edge to the trailing or posterior edge. There are several large transverse white photophores on the ventral surface. The coloration of these fishes is distinctive: the body is a light gray-blue, the shoulder organ is black, and in the juveniles the caudal peduncle or tail lacks pigment.

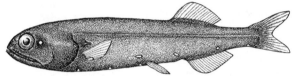

Fig. 2. *Sagamichthys abei*

Natural history notes. — *Sagamichthys abei* occurs throughout the north Pacific Ocean and in the eastern south Pacific Ocean, and is the most abundant of all the searsiids. The largest individual is almost 13 inches long. The otoliths from a 10-inch individual had only three winter zones, indicating that the shining tubeshoulder may be a short-lived species, or that large adults are not being captured by any type of fishing gear used to date.

The tubeshoulder undergoes a series of remarkable changes during its life history. Young and juvenile individuals have a pigment pattern as described above. During this period, from larvae up to 6 inches in length, the fish continually gain in numbers of photophores. The white caudal peduncle gradually becomes pigmented. During growth from 6 to 8 inches every individual changes from a gray-blue bodied, white-tailed fish to dark brown or black. All individuals longer than 8 inches are densely pigmented, including the tail; the shoulder tube is easily overlooked. Additional photophores develop on the head after this metamorphosis of the large individuals.

The young of S. *abei* apparently migrate in association with *Cyclothone signata* to within 200 meters of the surface at night; they feed extensively on small crustaceans. Young individuals are common in the spring.

Fishery information. — Tubeshoulders are taken by deep-sea oceanographic trawling gear including midwater trawls and fine-mesh nets. Since these fish mainly occupy midwaters, they are not taken by bottom gear as alepocephalids are. Some tubeshoulders are found near the surface, usually at night; others have been taken well below 3,000 feet.

Other family members. — A recent familial revision distinguishes all known species. Besides *Sagamichthys* six species in five other genera occur off California. *Holtbyrnia* and *Maulisia* have photophores on the body; *Maulisia* has a large pit just in front of the shoulder tube, which is absent in *Holtbyrnia*. *Mirorictus*, *Normichthys*, and *Pellisolus* lack photophores. Several other characters must be investigated and counted to identify the various species.

Meaning of name. — *Sagamichthys* (fish of Sagami Bay, Japan) *abei* (for the noted Japanese ichthyologist, Tokiharu Abe).

ARGENTINIDAE (ARGENTINE FAMILY)
Pacific Argentine
Argentina sialis Gilbert

Distinguishing characters.— The Pacific argentine is distinguished from other midwater forms by the flat-sided silvery body covered with large, firmly attached scales. Other characters which are helpful in identifying this species are the large laterally directed eyes, the wedge-shaped head, and the anal fin originating well behind the dorsal — neither fin containing as many as 15 rays. The young have numerous darkly pigmented bars along the sides of their bodies.

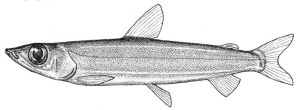

Fig. 3. *Argentina sialis*

Natural history notes. — *Argentina sialis* ranges from the vicinity of Eureka to and into the Gulf of California, but is not commonly caught anywhere within this area. Its rarity is probably due to lack of fishing effort in its preferred habitat rather than from a shortage of individuals. Catch records indicate that it lives in close association with the bottom: numerous individuals have been obtained during otter-trawling operations in Santa Monica Bay, and with explosives during seismic exploration for oil in other parts of the California borderland. During descents of diving saucers off southern California, small aggregations of Pacific argentines were photographed "fluttering" around near the bottom in 600 to 900 feet of water.

A 7-inch female weighing two ounces was five years old, judged by the rings on its otoliths. The largest individual known, a ripe female, was just over 8 inches long and weighed about three and a half ounces. Off our coast, spawning apparently begins in January and continues into spring months; ripe males have been captured in mid-October, however.

Pacific argentines are frequently found in the stomachs of rockfishes (*Sebastodes* spp.) or are spit up by rockfishes in their dying gasps. Although almost any type of food that would fit its mouth could be eaten by *A. sialis,* only crustacean remains have been found in their stomachs.

A single fossil otolith of *A. sialis* has been found in a Pleistocene deposit at Playa del Rey.

Fishery information. — The Pacific argentine has been taken with explosives, midwater trawls, and bottom trawls, and from the stomachs of other fishes. Best catches have been made with gear that has fished at or near the bottom; the species is rarely caught in midwater trawling operations. All the other members of the family are most abundant at mid-depths. A *Nansenia* that washed ashore on a beach south of San Francisco represents one of the few records of a member of this family other than *Argentina* being taken without midwater gear.

Other family members. — Five genera are currently recognized in the family Argentinidae: *Argentina, Glossanodon, Nansenia, Microstoma,* and *Xenophthalmichthys.* Only three (*Argentina, Microstoma,* and *Nansenia*) occur off California. *Nansenia* and *Microstoma* at first glance seem similar in basic body plan but *Nansenia* is not as elongate, has an adipose fin, and its ventral fins originate behind the anterior end of the dorsal fin base. The two species of *Nansenia* which occur off our coast may be distinguished by their color: *N. candida* is bright and silvery; *N. crassa* is dull and blackish.

Meaning of name. — *Argentina* (of silvery color, in reference to the body coloration), *sialis* (pertaining to a bird; the long, sharp snout may have looked like a bird's beak to the describer).

BATHYLAGIDAE (BLACKSMELT FAMILY)
Pacific Blacksmelt
Bathylagus pacificus Gilbert

Distinguishing characters. — The Pacific blacksmelt has large eyes, deciduous scales, a single dorsal fin, and a long anal fin far back on the body which distinguishes it from other fishes in our waters. The mouth is quite small and contains very weak dentition. The large operculum extends high up on the body (to the lateral line). There are only two branchiostegal rays, which is typical of the family.

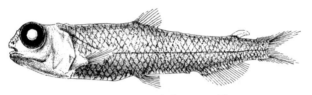

Fig. 4. *Bathylagus pacificus*

Natural history notes. — *Bathylagus pacificus* is found only in the eastern north Pacific Ocean; it ranges from the Gulf of Alaska to northern Baja California (at least). Two other members of the family, *B. stilbius* and *B. wesethi,* are much more common off California. *Bathylagus pacificus* lives at depths considerably greater than 1,000 feet, and does not undertake a diurnal, vertical migration. A full-grown individual is about 10 inches long and weighs around four ounces. Otoliths of a *B. pacificus* about 6 inches long had five winter rings; those from several 4½-inch fish had three. Ripe eggs have been noted in the ovaries of blacksmelt during the spring. Pacific blacksmelt and most other members of the family feed heavily on crustaceans. Blacksmelt are eaten by numerous larger predators living in the same environment.

Bathylagus remains, including entire compressed skeletons, have been found in many Miocene diatomite and shale deposits in southern California, and the otoliths of some species (not *B. pacificus*) are abundant in several Pliocene and Miocene deposits.

Fishery information. — Most specimens of *B. pacificus* taken off California have been captured with midwater trawls and other deep-sea sampling gear operated from research vessels. A close relative, *B. stilbius,* is one of the commonest midwater fishes in the California fauna. In a four-hour tow with a ten-foot midwater trawl in the San Pedro Basin, more than 16,000 specimens of *B. stilbius* were captured. Individuals of several species are regularly taken near the surface at night. These fishes are known to occur at depths exceeding 3,000 feet.

Other family members. — All members of the family belong to the genus *Bathylagus*. Six species are known from off California. Two species (*milleri* and *pacificus*) are large and black and have deciduous scales; *B. milleri* has more anal fin rays than *B. pacificus*. *Bathylagus stilbius* has a pointed snout, and its color in life is iridescent. Of the remaining three species, *B. ochotensis* has scales over most of its body, whereas scales are never seen on either *B. wesethi* or *B. nigrigenys; B. nigrigenys* has a deeper body (18 to 21.5 percent of standard length) than *B. wesethi* (16.5 to 19 percent).

Meaning of name. — *Bathylagus* (hare coming from the deep sea, in reference to the peculiar mouth and teeth) *pacificus* (pertaining to the Pacific Ocean, its habitat).

OPISTHOPROCTIDAE (SPOOKFISH FAMILY)
Brownsnout Spookfish
Dolichopteryx longipes (Vaillant)

Distinguishing characters. — Brownsnout spookfish are slender and elongate, have tubular eyes, and lack pigment on the body, but have a brown stripe on the snout. They are further distinguished by the extremely gelatinous skin, the small dorsal fin well in advance of the anal fin, and the long snout. Spookfish are so delicate that they are usually mutilated by collecting gear.

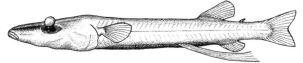

Fig. 5. *Dolichopteryx longipes*

Natural history notes. — Relatively few spookfish and their allies are known from any ocean, including the eastern Pacific off California. *Dolichopteryx longipes,* the commonest member of the family, apparently is cosmopolitan in distribution. They evidently do not live at great depths; brownsnout spookfish are regularly taken at depths shallower than 1,500 feet off southern California. A very large individual would measure six inches long, and would probably weigh less than a writing pencil. The otoliths of a 5-inch individual had five winter rings; this was the largest fish from which we had otoliths.

Spookfish feed mostly on small crustaceans, particularly copepods. The small peculiar jaws and teeth of *D. longipes* appear to be very inefficient for capturing rapidly moving organisms.

Fishery information. — Opisthoproctids have been taken only with scientific deep-sea fishing gear. Plankton nets and other small-mesh nets have yielded some of the least-damaged specimens.

Other family members. — Of the six known opisthoproctid genera, only four occur off California. The elongate slender-bodied genera, *Dolichopteryx* and *Bathylychnops,* are easily distinguished, and the tubular eyes of *Dolichopteryx* separate it from *Bathylychnops.* Two short, fat-bodied genera are also represented in the California fauna. The ventral surface of *Opisthoproctus* is flat and ironlike in appearance,

[25]

and may be luminescent. *Macropinna* has neither the flattened venter nor the luminescence, but does have typical upturned tubular or barrel-like eyes.

Meaning of name. — *Dolichopteryx* (long wings, in reference to the long pectoral and pelvic fin rays) *longipes* (also, in reference to the long pelvics).

GONOSTOMATIDAE (LIGHTFISH FAMILY)
Benttooth Bristlemouth
Cyclothone acclinidens Garman
and
Bigeye Lightfish
Danaphos oculatus (Garman)

Distinguishing characters. — Lightfishes are generally characterized by having true gill rakers, small teeth (no enlarged fangs), serial photophores with lumen or a duct, an elongate body, and more or less horizontal jaws. Few exceed 3 inches when full grown, and many never attain 2 inches. The family is large and complex, but may be divided into two subgroups: one contains fishes in which the serial photophores are separate; in the other the serial photophores are grouped in common glands appearing as black or silvery bands. We have illustrated one member of each group to aid in recognition. *Cyclothone* (serial

Fig. 6. *Cyclothone acclinidens*

photophores separate) reminds one of a cartoonist's version of a fish skeleton, which has been enveloped in a thin, semitransparent layer of parchment. *Cyclothone acclinidens* is the only bristlemouth in which all the teeth on the maxillary are set at angles of about 45°, with each tooth about the same size as the one next to it. *Danaphos* can be distinguished by its photophore arrangement, body shape, and unpigmented, semitransparent body.

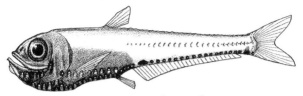

Fig. 7. *Danaphos oculatus*

Natural history notes. — *C. acclinidens* apparently is found in most oceans of the world; in the eastern Pacific it ranges from mid-Oregon to central Chile (at least). Numerically, some members of this genus probably are the most abundant fishes in the world, but because of their small size and the depth at which they live (usually 1,000 feet or more beneath the surface) they probably will never contribute directly to man's food supply. A full-grown specimen of *C. acclinidens* would not be as long as a kitchen match and would not weigh half as much. Otoliths from large, mature individuals have two or three winter rings; we have not seen any with four rings. The benttooth bristlemouth and most of the other members of the family we have investigated feed heavily upon small crustaceans. Bristlemouths are eaten by larger predators living in the same environment, sometimes in great quantities. We have noted ripe eggs in their ovaries during spring months off our coast.

Cyclothone remains, including entire compressed skeletons, have been found in many Miocene diatomite and shale deposits in southern California.

Danaphos oculatus has been reported from throughout much of the eastern north Pacific Ocean (Oregon to Panama) and from the Indian Ocean. It also lives quite deep (1,200 feet or more beneath the surface), and, judged by frequency of occurrence in net hauls made in its environment, is nowhere near as abundant as *Cyclothone*. A 2¼-inch specimen of *Danaphos* could be considered a giant, for captured individuals seldom exceed 1½ inches. The otoliths of a very large specimen had five winter rings, but no other otoliths among twenty sets examined had more than three rings.

Fishery information. — The only certain way to catch either of these species is with a fine-meshed midwater trawl towed 1,000 to 2,000 feet or more beneath the surface. Remains of both have been found in the stomachs of deep-feeding fishes such as lancetfish.

Other family members. — At least sixteen species of lightfishes belonging to seven genera are known from off California (the genus *Cyclothone* with seven species is the most prolific). *Danaphos* and *Valenciennellus* have serial photophores grouped in common glands, whereas in the other five genera the serial photophores are separate. Three of the five, *Vinciguerria*, *Woodsia*, and *Ichthyococcus*, have photophores on the isthmus, but the other two, *Gonostoma* and *Cyclothone*, do not. Numerous characters must be investigated, measured, and counted in order to identify all the various genera and species.

Meaning of names. — *Cyclothone* (circle veil, apparently in allusion to the veil-like body covering) *acclinidens* (slanted teeth). *Danaphos* (Dana lighted, or a lighted fish first captured by the research vessel *Dana*) *oculatus* (having eyes).

STERNOPTYCHIDAE (HATCHETFISH FAMILY)
Pacific Hatchetfish
Argyropelecus pacificus Schultz

Distinguishing characters. — The compressed, hatchet-shaped body, the tubular eyes directed skyward, and the straight alignment of the ventral row of photophores (supra-abdominal, preanal, anal, and subcaudal) distinguish the Pacific hatchetfish from all other fishes in our waters.

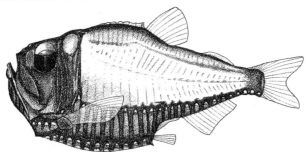

Fig. 8. *Argyropelecus pacificus*

Natural history notes. — *Argyropelecus pacificus* ranges throughout the eastern Pacific Ocean from Oregon to below the equator and offshore to Hawaii. It has never been observed at the surface, but is abundant in scattering layers several hundred to several thousand feet beneath the surface. A possible record-sized individual was 4 inches long, but specimens longer than 3½ inches are rare. The otoliths of several 2½- to 3-inch specimens showed three to four winter zones, which were believed to be indicative of their age. Data are not at hand regarding maximum age and spawning habits. An examination of numerous stomachs revealed an assortment of small crustaceans and an occasional tiny larval fish. Hatchetfish, in turn, are preyed upon by many larger predatory fishes, sometimes in considerable quantity.

Fossil skeletons of *Argyropelecus* have been found imbedded in Miocene age diatomites at several localities in California; some of these may be *A. pacificus.*

Fishery information. — Hatchetfishes are usually caught in midwater trawls or found in the stomachs of predatory fishes. Commercial and sport fishermen frequently report individuals that have been regurgitated by albacore, but lancetfishes and rockfishes also have been known to feed upon hatchetfishes. *Argyropelecus pacificus* was among the many fish species killed in 1950 when lava from the erupting Mauna Loa flowed into the sea.

Other family members. — Four other hatchetfishes are known to our coast: *Sternoptyx diaphana, Argyropelecus intermedius, A. lychnus,* and *A. hawaiensis.* *Sternoptyx* has normally positioned eyes on each side of the head, whereas in *Argyropelecus* the eyes are tubular and directed upward. *Argyropelecus intermedius* has a single, rather elongate postabdominal spine; all other *Argyropelecus* have a pair of small, slightly diverging postabdominal spines. The upper preopercular spine of *A. hawaiensis* curves outward, upward, and backward, but in *A. lychnus* it curves outward, downward, and backward.

Meaning of name. — *Argyropelecus* (silvery hatchet) *pacificus* (Pacific, for the area it inhabits).

STOMIATIDAE (SCALY DRAGONFISH FAMILY)
Blackbelly Dragonfish
Stomias atriventer Garman

Distinguishing characters. — The blackbelly dragonfish is the only elongate blackish fish in our waters that has a luminous-tipped mental barbel (chin whisker), sides covered with hexagonal pigmented areas which form scalelike patterns, and a dorsal fin originating well back along the body.

Fig. 9. *Stomias atriventer*

Natural history notes. — *Stomias atriventer*, which ranges from the vicinity of central California to that of mid-Mexico, is especially abundant throughout the deep areas of the Gulf of California. Except at night,

[30]

when some individuals can be captured within 500 feet of the surface, blackbelly dragonfishes usually remain at depths of 1,000 feet or more. The largest of more than a hundred individuals seen over a period of several years was a little over 10 inches long. Although the otoliths are difficult to interpret, an examination of more than a dozen sets leads us to believe that they attain an age of at least five years. The stomachs of those we examined contained mainly crustaceans and lanternfishes. In our area most spawning occurs in the spring, but no data are available on larval stages.

Fishery information. — We do not know of any blackbelly dragonfishes being found in stomachs of predatory species. They are easily taken with fine-meshed midwater trawls that are fished 1,000 feet or more beneath the surface, but few tows yield more than a single fish unless fishing is in a relatively restricted zone 2,000 to 2,600 feet down. Tows made within this belt of water often catch twenty or more specimens of *S. atriventer.*

Other family members. — No other member of the family is known within several thousand miles of California.

Meaning of name. — *Stomias* (mouthy) *atriventer* (black belly).

MELANOSTOMIATIDAE (SCALELESS DRAGON-FISH FAMILY)
Highfin Dragonfish
Bathophilus flemingi Aron and McCrery

Distinguishing characters. — Because the dorsal fin originates at the same point far back on the body as the anal fin (except for *Flagellostomias* in our waters), it is difficult to mistake these black, scaleless, bathypelagic fishes for any except perhaps *Aristostomias* or, if the skin is missing, *Stomias.* Scaleless dragonfishes are more slender and toothy than scaly dragon-

[31]

fishes, and are easily distinguished from *Aristostomias* by the way in which the head is attached. The high-fin dragonfish can be distinguished from other scale-less dragonfishes by the very elongate pelvic fins which are attached on the midsides, and by the serial photophores in deep pits.

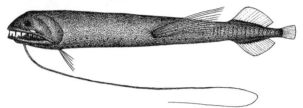

Fig. 10. *Bathophilus flemingi*

Natural history notes.—*Bathophilus flemingi* ranges from off British Columbia to somewhere off central Baja California (at least). At night, adults have been caught within 600 feet of the surface, but daylight catches are heaviest at three times that depth or deeper. Maximum length for the species is about 6 inches, and an examination of several sets of otoliths indicates that they live perhaps eight years. Spawning apparently occurs in spring and early summer. The stomachs of those we examined contained small crustaceans almost exclusively. Scaleless dragonfishes, probably including *Bathophilus*, are eaten by many predatory species that inhabit the same depths, or travel there to feed.

Fishery information. — Most if not all specimens of *B. flemingi* on record were captured with midwater trawls and in similar gear operated from research vessels. They probably are moderately common, but few net hauls yield more than a single individual.

Other family members. — Six other scaleless dragonfishes have been caught off California. Among these, *Flagellostomias* has an anal fin that originates ahead of the dorsal fin, whereas in all other genera the anal and dorsal fins originate at about the same point. In *Opostomias* the first mandibular tooth pierces the premaxillary (not so in the remaining four). *Tactostoma* (with a toothless vomer) and *Photonectes* (with a toothed vomer) have an upward-curving lower jaw that is longer than the upper; in *Melanostomias* (with a toothed vomer) and *Bathophilus* (vomer without teeth) the lower jaw is not longer than the upper and is not curved. *Bathophilus brevis* has winglike ventral fins in that they are attached high on the body near the dorsal profile, and has a very deep, almost oval body.

Meaning of name. — *Bathophilus* (literally deep love; a fish that loves the depths) *flemingi* (for Richard H. Fleming, noted oceanographer).

MALACOSTEIDAE (LOOSEJAW FAMILY)
Shiny Loosejaw
Aristostomias scintillans (Gilbert)

Distinguishing characters. — The shiny loosejaw is the only blackish scaleless fish in our waters that has no floor to its mouth. The posteriorly placed dorsal and anal fins, the fairly long mental barbel (chin whisker) that terminates in a distinct luminous bulb, and the fact that the head connects to the body high up in the neck region assist in rapid identification.

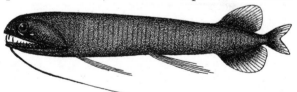

Fig. 11. *Aristostomias scintillans*

Natural history notes. — *Aristostomias scintillans* ranges from southern British Columbia to central Baja California (at least), and offshore for several hundred miles. Occasional individuals are netted as close to the surface as 500 feet, and one has been reported from 100 feet, but most captures are made at depths greater than 1,000 feet. It is unusual to see a shiny loosejaw that exceeds 6 inches in length, but there is at least one reliable report of a 9-incher. The largest of nearly a dozen pairs of otoliths we examined had seven winter annuli, indicating that the fish, a 7-incher, was in its eighth year. An examination of several stomachs indicates that *A. scintillans* prefers crustaceans above all else. The presence of ripening ovaries in some of the large females indicates that spawning occurs in the spring, but nothing is known about hatching time or larval life.

Fishery information. — To our knowledge, *A. scintillans* has been captured only with midwater trawls and similar nets being towed by research vessels in their investigations of offshore waters.

Other family members. — No other member of the family is known within several thousand miles of California.

Meaning of name. — *Aristostomias* (noblest *Stomias*) *scintillans* (sparkly, in allusion to the glittering photophores).

IDIACANTHIDAE (BLACKDRAGON FAMILY)
Pacific Blackdragon
Idiacanthus antrostomus Gilbert

Distinguishing characters. — The long, slender, scaleless body, the long dorsal and anal fins, and a pair of short, pointed, bony projections anterior to and flanking the base of each dorsal and anal ray distinguish adult blackdragons from all other fishes in our waters. Female blackdragons differ greatly from the males: they attain much larger sizes, are dark black (males are brownish), have prominent fanglike teeth (jaws of males lack teeth); an elongate barbel, or chin whisker (lacking in males), pelvic fins (absent in males), and a functional digestive tract (nonfunctional in males). The colorless larvae have eyes at the tips of elongate stalks.

Fig. 12.   *Idiacanthus antrostomus*

Natural history notes. — *Idiacanthus antrostomus* ranges throughout most of the tropic and temperate eastern Pacific Ocean, both north and south of the equator. These fish migrate toward the surface at night, and return to the depths at dawn. Females attain lengths of 15 inches or more, but a recently reported "giant" male was only 3 inches long. A 13-inch female, weighing slightly less than one ounce, was six years old judged by the rings on its otoliths. A 14½-inch female also weighed less than one ounce but its age was not determined. In view of the nonfunctional digestive tract of the male, its life span is undoubtedly completed in less than twelve months. Blackdragons are most abundant in our waters during spring and summer, which apparently corresponds with their spawning season. Small fishes and an assortment of crustaceans make up the bulk of their diet. These are usually pretty well chewed before being swallowed. A large female Atlantic blackdragon was reported to have had 14,000 nearly mature eggs in her ovaries.

Fishery information. — Pacific blackdragons are rarely found in the stomachs of predatory fishes, but are caught fairly commonly in fine-meshed midwater trawls. Larvae and juveniles are sometimes taken with plankton nets.

Other family members. — No other members of the family are known within several thousand miles of California.

Meaning of name. — *Idiacanthus* (peculiar spine, with reference to the pair of short spiny projections anterior to and flanking the base of each dorsal and anal fin ray) *antrostomus* (cavern mouth).

CHAULIODONTIDAE (VIPERFISH FAMILY)
Pacific Viperfish
Chauliodus macouni Bean

Distinguishing characters. — The very long, fang-like anterior jaw teeth that remain outside the mouth, the hexagonal pigmented areas (each covered by a scale) along the sides of the body, and the dorsal fin originating well in advance of the pelvic fins distinguish the Pacific viperfish from all other fishes in our area.

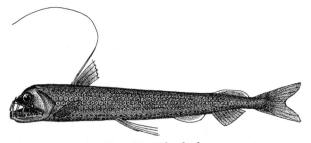

Fig. 13. *Chauliodus macouni*

Natural history notes. — *Chauliodus macouni* ranges from the Gulf of Alaska to waters off central Baja California at depths of 250 to 5,000 feet. Captures in shallow water are unusual, and those reported for the greatest depths may be in error because the nets could have picked them up anywhere between the surface and maximum depth during setting and retrieving. The species never attains a large size: a length of about 9 inches and a weight of one ounce are maximums. Growth zones observed on numerous otoliths indicate that some individuals attain ages of at least eight years. *Chauliodus* is strictly carnivorous, feeding mainly upon small fishes but also upon crustaceans and squids. The filamentous first dorsal fin ray is apparently used as an angling device (attractant or lure) because those noted from diving saucers always have this fin ray curved forward with the tip before and above the mouth, but prey capture has not been observed. Data on other phases of life history are not available.

Fossil remains of *Chauliodus* (entire skeletal imprints) are not uncommon in several Miocene diatomite and shale deposits in southern California. These represent an extinct species, *C. eximius*. In some specimens, the remains of their last meals have been preserved intact.

Fishery information. — *Chauliodus* is rarely caught by other than midwater trawls fished 1,000 feet or more beneath the surface. An occasional viperfish is caught with bottom trawling gear using small-mesh liners or bags, but these may have been taken as the net was on its way down or up rather than on the bottom. We do not know of any viperfish being found in the stomachs of larger predators, but they are probably eaten by predators that can catch them in their natural environment.

Other family members. — No other member of the family is known within several thousand miles of California.

Meaning of name. — *Chauliodus* (exserted tooth) *macouni* (for Professor John C. Macoun of the Geological Survey of Canada).

ASTRONESTHIDAE (SNAGGLETOOTH FAMILY)
Panama Snaggletooth
Borostomias panamensis Regan and Trewavas

Distinguishing characters. — The origin of the dorsal fin well in advance of the anal fin origin, the evenly spaced photophores along the belly, mental barbel (chin whisker) with a bulb five times as long as it is wide, and 17 to 19 anal fin rays distinguish the black scaleless Panama snaggletooth from all other species in our waters.

Fig. 14. *Borostomias panamensis*

Natural history notes. — *Borostomias panamensis* ranges from the vicinity of Point Conception to south of Panama. Juveniles, or at least the smallest individuals, are usually caught at shallower depths than adults. Few large individuals have been netted closer to the surface than about 1,500 feet, but from there to perhaps 3,000 feet occasional captures are made. The maximum known size for *B. panamensis* seems to be just over 12 inches, but the species may grow even larger. Otoliths of half a dozen individuals were examined, but even the largest of these (from a 10-inch fish) had only five winter rings. Thus the species may be short-lived, or the largest adults are escaping capture. Almost nothing is known of other phases of life history or of food habits. Although the stomachs we examined contained mostly crustaceans, *B. panamensis* will probably eat small fishes, mollusks, worms, and other food when these are the easiest to capture.

Fishery information. — We do not know of any snaggletooth captures except those made with fine-mesh midwater trawls and similar nets operated from research vessels. Stomachs of deep-feeding predators are logical places to find their remains, and as food-habit studies are conducted on such predators (sword-fish, some tunas, lancetfishes, etc.) *Borostomias* should turn up occasionally.

Other family members. — Only one other member of the family, *Neonesthes capensis*, has been reported from off California, and it has been noted only once. The 25 to 28 anal rays of *Neonesthes* easily distinguish it from *Borostomias*, which usually has only 17 to 19 anal rays.

Meaning of name. — *Borostomias* (greedy *Stomias*) *panamensis* (belonging to Panama, the locality of first capture for the species).

BATHYLACONIDAE (BONYTHROAT FAMILY)
Bonythroat
Bathylaco nigricans Goode and Bean

Distinguishing characters. — At first glance this small, black, very rare bathypelagic fish seems to resemble a myctophid without photophores, or an ale-pocephalid, but a closer look reveals that the bran-chiostegal rays of the bonythroat are platelike and fully exposed, a characteristic not possessed by other fishes. The uppermost branchiostegal ray is attached

Fig. 15. *Bathylaco nigricans*

to opercular bones along two margins, whereas suc-ceeding rays are attached to the ray above and to one of the opercular bones anteriorly. There is a narrow, slightly crescentic, luminescent organ in front of each eye; otherwise photophores are lacking.

Natural history notes. — *Bathylaco nigricans* is known from fewer than a dozen specimens, most of them from the Atlantic Ocean and two (at least) from the Pacific. One of the Pacific specimens was netted off Colombia and the other off southern California. Netted specimens of *B. nigricans* have come from fishing operations conducted in waters as shallow as 2,000 feet and as deep as 15,000 feet. At just under 11 inches the bonythroat from off our coast is the largest known. Apparently this fish is an adult, but no information is available regarding age, spawning habits, food, or other phases of its life history.

Fishery information. — Most of the known bonythroats were caught with midwater trawls at great depths; one was found in the stomach of a deep-living predatory fish that had been caught on hook and line well beneath the surface of the sea.

Other family members. — No other member of the family is known.

Meaning of name. — *Bathylaco* (deep hole or pit, possibly in reference to the depth at which the net was being towed when it captured the first one) *nigricans* (blackish).

GIGANTURIDAE (TELESCOPEFISH FAMILY)
Pacific Telescopefish
Bathyleptus lisae Walters

Distinguishing characters. — The large forward-directed tubular eyes, the very large mouth lined with strongly curved teeth, the fanlike pectoral fins inserted horizontally above the gill openings, and the elongate lower lobe on the forked caudal fin are sufficient to distinguish this strangest of strange-looking fishes. The Pacific telescopefish lacks pelvic fins, scales, and luminous organs, and the body has a jelly-like layer beneath the skin.

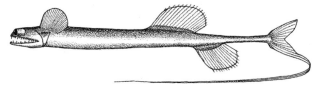

Fig. 16.   *Bathyleptus lisae*

Natural history notes. — Fewer than ten specimens of *Bathyleptus lisae* are known. Future deep-trawling expeditions undoubtedly will expand its known range, but at present, individuals have been taken only off southern California, northern Baja California, north of the Hawaiian Islands, and between Chile and New Zealand in the southern hemisphere. The largest of those captured to date was slightly less than 8 inches long to the base of its tail. The otoliths of a 6-inch fish had three winter rings. No details are available on spawning habits, food, or predators. Scientists at La Jolla have recently found that the larva of *Bathyleptus* is even more peculiar-looking than the adult; this accounts for its previous description under a different generic name and the failure to associate it with the telescopefishes.

Fishery information. — All known adults have been captured in midwater trawls during exploratory fishing operations by scientific personnel from several universities and organizations. Successful hauls have yielded *B. lisae* from waters as shallow as 2,000 feet and as deep as 12,000 feet.

Other family members. — No other member of the family is known within many thousands of miles of California. The only other genus in the family, *Gigantura,* can be recognized by its caudal peduncle, which is one and a half times as deep as it is wide (in *Ba-*

thyleptus it is as wide as or wider than it is deep).

Meaning of name. — *Bathyleptus* (deep slender, in reference to the depth range of capture and its body shape) *lisae* (for Lisa, the wife of the scientist who described the species).

NEOSCOPELIDAE (BLACKCHIN FAMILY)
Pacific Blackchin
Scopelengys tristis Alcock

Distinguishing characters. — The small eye, large mouth, and wedge-shaped head of this large-scaled blackish fish usually preclude misidentification. Even though the scales are usually missing, the scale pockets indicate their size. The Pacific blackchin closely resembles certain of the lanternfishes (Myctophidae), but has no photophores.

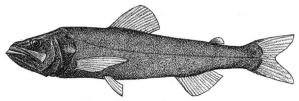

Fig. 17.   *Scopelengys tristis*

Natural history notes. — *Scopelengys tristis* is known throughout much of the tropic and temperate Pacific and Indian oceans, ranging from the vicinity of Santa Barbara to mid-Chile (18° S.) in the eastern Pacific. Although a few individuals may stray to within 1,500 feet of the surface, the greatest concentrations seem to occur below 2,000 feet, but even at these great depths they are not caught abundantly. Maximum length for a blackchin is 8 inches or slightly more, and maximum weight just over an ounce. The largest of ten pairs of otoliths examined for indications of age had six winter rings; these were from a fish a little more than 7 inches long. Their food consists mainly of small crustaceans. In our area spawning apparently takes place during late spring.

Fishery information. — To our knowledge, all known specimens of S. *tristis* have been captured by research vessels using midwater trawls and similar gear. They should be a choice food for large predators living in their environment, but we do not know of their remains having been found in the stomachs of other fish.

Other family members. — No other member of the family is known within several thousand miles of California.

Meaning of name. — *Scopelengys* (near *Scopelus,* in reference to its resemblance to *Scopelus,* a genus of lanternfishes) *tristis* (dull, alluding to its dull blackish color).

MYCTOPHIDAE (LANTERNFISH FAMILY)
California Lanternfish
Symbolophorus californiensis
(Eigenmann and Eigenmann)

Distinguishing characters. — The California lanternfish is distinguished from other lanternfishes by its soft and flexible procurrent caudal rays, the AO photophores (the row at the base of the anal fin on each side) in two series, a single Pol (the photophore between the adipose fin and the AO), the absence of photophores above or in the lateral line, the anal fin base longer than that of the dorsal fin, each VO series

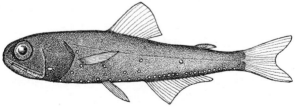

Fig. 18. *Symbolophorus californiensis*

[43]

(those between the ventral fin base and the anal fin insertion) in a straight line, and the SAO (three photophores on the midside) forming a right angle. It is the only member of the genus in our waters.

Natural history notes. — *Symbolophorus californiensis* ranges from northern British Columbia to the vicinity of Cedros Island, Baja California, and offshore for several hundred miles. At maximum size, about 5 inches, an individual weighs slightly over half an ounce. The age of a 4-inch fish, based upon growth zones on its otoliths, was five years, so some individuals may reach the age of seven years. In our waters at least three other lanternfishes (*Parvilux ingens, Lampanyctus regalis,* and *Lampadena urophaos*) attain larger maximum sizes, but data on their potential ages are not available. Most lanternfishes seem to live for three to five years, and some may live as long as seven or eight years. The California lanternfish spawns during spring and summer (as do most lanternfishes in our waters), and feeds almost exclusively upon small crustaceans. Fossil lanternfish "imprints" (skeletal remains) are abundant in Miocene diatomite and shale deposits throughout much of southern California, and myctophid otoliths, including those of *Symbolophorus,* have been found in a dozen or more Pleistocene, Pliocene, and Miocene deposits.

Fishery information. — *S. californiensis* is easily attracted to a light suspended above the water at night, and many are captured in dipnets. They have been taken in abundance with midwater trawling gear, and occasional individuals have been found in the stomachs of such predatory species as albacore, jack mackerel, and rockfish. Most types of fishing gear, including hook and line, have been successful in capturing lanternfishes, and the stomachs of many marine mammals, birds, and cephalopods often yield quantities of lanternfishes and lanternfish remains.

Sometimes catastrophic die-offs occur and tens of thousands of dead lanternfishes drift ashore or are observed floating at the surface in offshore areas, presumably victims of drastic temperature changes or other lethal phenomena.

Other family members. — More than thirty other lanternfishes belonging to twenty genera have been noted from waters off California. Myctophids and gonostomatids are the most abundant bathypelagic finfishes in the world oceans. Because of their small size, it is not likely that they will provide first-order protein to save the starving multitudes of an overpopulated world.

Numerous external characters are helpful in distinguishing lanternfish genera and species, but their photophores (number, placement, size, patterns formed, etc.) are by far the most used and useful. In recent years, myctophid specialists have split up established genera and species so often that it has been difficult for the average ichthyologist to keep pace with the changes, much less evaluate them.

Meaning of name. — *Symbolophorus* (bearer of a symbol or sign, with reference to the strongly angulated SAO which distinguishes it from *Myctophum*) *californiensis* (belonging to California).

PARALEPIDIDAE (BARRACUDINA FAMILY)
Slender Barracudina
Lestidium ringens (Jordan and Gilbert)

Distinguishing characters. — If body shape, fin position and length, and dentition are taken into consideration, no other fish in our waters can be mistaken for a barracudina. It has an elongate body, scaleless except for the lateral line, and a longitudinal luminous duct on the midventral line between the head and the paired ventral fins. The slender barracudina seems to be the only paralepidid with tubes on the lateral line, and has the shortest snout of any barracudina in our waters (head 2.0 to 2.2 times as long as snout).

Fig. 19. *Lestidium ringens*

Natural history notes. — *Lestidium ringens,* an oceanic species, ranges from off British Columbia to the vicinity of Cedros Island, Baja California. It is sometimes caught within a few hundred feet of the surface, but most individuals inhabit depths of 1,000 to 1,500 feet or more. The largest specimens caught are about 8 inches long and weigh about one-tenth of an ounce. The otoliths of a 7⅛-inch fish indicated that it was just over four years old, but no information is available on ages of other specimens, either larger or smaller. The few stomachs that have been examined indicate a diet mostly of small fish including larvae of other species, but small crustaceans and cephalopods also were found, especially in young individuals. Barracudinas are fed upon rather extensively by such predatory species as albacore, salmon, swordfish, and lancetfish. Barracudina otoliths were recovered from the stomach of a squid, along with other fish remains.

Lestidium-like fossils have been found in Miocene diatomite at Lompoc, California.

Fishery information. — Albacore and salmon fishermen commonly find barracudinas that have been spit up on deck by fish they have caught. Most of these specimens are small, 3 to 4 inches long, but 6-inch barracudinas have also been noted with regularity. Midwater trawls and plankton nets probably yield most of the remaining barracudinas that are captured each year, but any fine-meshed net being used in offshore waters could take an occasional specimen.

Other family members. — At least six other paralepidids belonging to four additional genera are known from off California. The adults of two of these, *Paralepis* (with 17 pectoral fin rays) and *Notolepis* (with 10 to 12 pectoral rays), are easily distinguished because their bodies are completely scaled. Among the scaleless barracudinas, *Sudis* has a massive head and the margins of its jaw teeth are finely serrate; *Macroparalepis* has 25 or fewer anal fin rays, and *Lestidium* has 26 or more. The heads of the two last-named genera are not massive and the jaw teeth are not serrate.

Meaning of name. — *Lestidium* (a little pirate or robber) *ringens* (gaping, in allusion to the large mouth).

ALEPISAURIDAE (LANCETFISH FAMILY)
Longnose lancetfish
Alepisaurus ferox Lowe

Distinguishing characters. — Although the barracuda-like body topped with a sailfish-like fin distinguishes the lancetfish from all other denizens of the deep, the longnose lancetfish received its common name from its lancelike fangs. The skull bones are thin and papery, and the translucent skin which covers the body is without scales.

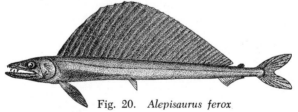

Fig. 20. *Alepisaurus ferox*

Natural history notes. — *Alepisaurus ferox* is fairly abundant in the eastern Pacific Ocean between British Columbia and Chile, and offshore to and beyond the Hawaiian Islands. It is abundant also throughout most of the western Pacific, Indian, and Atlantic oceans. The largest of several hundred specimens examined in recent years was 5 feet 3 inches long; it weighed almost ten pounds, as did a 4-foot 2-inch individual caught off Fort Bragg, California.

One of the most interesting features of the lancetfish is its voracious appetite. In spite of their impressive dentures, lancetfish seldom mutilate their prey; the fishes and other creatures found in their stomachs are usually in near-perfect condition. Many descriptions of new (to science) fish, octopus, and squid species have been based upon items found in lancetfish stomachs.

Off California, more than thirty kinds of fishes, ten kinds of squids and octopuses, eight kinds of pteropods and heteropods (pelagic mollusks), ten kinds of pelagic amphipods (crustaceans), three kinds of polychaete worms, and five kinds of tunicates, salps, ctenophores, and jellyfish have been fed upon by lancetfish that were caught on longline gear. Off New Caledonia, 31 longline-caught lancetfish had eaten an average of 48.6 cubic centimeters of food representing 21 organisms. Fishes were most important among these, contributing 47 percent by volume and 40 percent by numbers. A single lancetfish (caught about 300 miles off California) had eaten, as a last meal, 41 fishes of five kinds, three cephalopods of two kinds, one amphipod, and one polychaete worm. Another lancetfish caught near the Galapagos Islands had eaten 81 inch-long hatchetfish before taking a baited hook. Many lancetfish are cannibalistic, and as many as seven young have been found in the stomach of a larger individual.

Possibly because of their voracious appetite, lancetfish are often heavily parasitized. At least four kinds of larval tapeworms have been found in their flesh and viscera, as well as one kind of trematode (fluke) and one adult tapeworm.

Besides being preyed upon by their own kind, lancetfish are eaten by opahs, sharks, and albacore and yellowfin tunas. Off New Caledonia, at least half of the longline-caught tunas (albacore or yellowfin) contained *Alepisaurus.*

Recent studies have shown that lancetfish are hermaphrodites: each individual contains both male and female reproductive organs. A large individual caught in an otter trawl off northern California in May showed indications that the spawning season was near. Precise information on the spawning season or spawning grounds is unavailable, as are data on growth rates and age.

Fishery information. — A fisherman or a beach stroller who sees a lancetfish swimming feebly in the surf may wade in, grab it by the tail, and head for shore. The usual reaction of the lancetfish is to attempt to bite large pieces from its captor. Less spectacular are the hundreds of captures on longline gear that is being fished primarily for tunas. An occasional sportfisherman will hook a lancetfish while he is fishing deep for albacore, and there is one record of a specimen being caught in an otter trawl.

Other family members. — *Alepisaurus ferox* is the only member of the family known off the California coast. In the Atlantic a smaller species, the shortnose lancetfish (*A. brevirostris*), is found over much of the range occupied by *A. ferox*

Meaning of name. — *Alepisaurus* (scaleless and lizard-like) *ferox* (ferocious).

ANOTOPTERIDAE (DAGGERTOOTH FAMILY)
Daggertooth
Anotopterus pharao Zugmayer

Distinguishing characters. — The elongate beaklike jaws filled with long bladelike teeth and vomerine teeth in the roof of the mouth which point forward are sufficient by themselves to identify the daggertooth. Added characters such as the prominent, sharp projection on the tip of the lower jaw (mandibular process) and the elongate, thin-skinned body, topped only with an adipose fin, will clinch its identification. On large individuals a few scales may be embedded along the sides of the body.

Fig. 21. *Anotopterus pharao*

Natural history notes. — Anotopterus pharao has an antitropical distribution; it is known from temperate and subpolar waters of both hemispheres but not from the tropics. Although the species was relatively unknown before the turn of the twentieth century, and was little known for nearly fifty years thereafter, it has turned up in increasing numbers each year since about the end of the Second World War. The first recorded occurrence off California was in 1952, but during the next twelve years perhaps a hundred were caught or found in our waters, including the world's largest — a 42-incher weighing almost three pounds, which was caught by a salmon troller in 1962. The otoliths of this fish had six winter rings, indicating that it was six years old if these rings can be assumed to be valid means of determining age.

Most daggertooths reported from our coast have been found in stomachs of albacore and lancetfish. In the Gulf of Alaska and south of the Aleutians, large specimens are occasionally caught in gill nets; others have been found in the stomachs of whales at the opposite end of the earth.

Daggertooths feed primarily on small fishes that inhabit the depths in which they live. Those from deep water usually have fed upon deep-sea fishes; those caught by salmon trollers usually contain small rockfishes, lingcod, and other surface-living juveniles. At least two small daggertooths were eaten by cannibalistic larger ones. A 4½-inch daggertooth found in the stomach of a lancetfish had in its stomach 16 half-inch lanternfish larvae.

No data are available on spawning habits, migratory patterns, or growth rates.

Fishery information. — Large individuals, 2 to 3 feet long, have been caught by fishermen trolling for salmon, usually 20 to 30 fathoms beneath the surface. Other specimens have been caught in gill nets, midwater trawls, and dipnets. Most of the daggertooths turned in by fishermen were found on the decks of their vessels where they were spit up by albacore, but some have been found in the stomachs of lancetfish and other daggertooths. In other parts of the world, halibut and whale stomachs have yielded daggertooths.

Other family members. — *A. pharao* is the sole member of the daggertooth family.

Meaning of name. —*Anotopterus* (lacking a dorsal fin) *pharao* (title of Egyptian kings).

SCOPELARCHIDAE (PEARLEYE FAMILY)
Longfin Pearleye
Benthalbella linguidens (Mead and Böhlke)

Distinguishing characters. — Pearleyes are easily distinguished by a glistening white spot on the side of a somewhat telescopic eye (directed forward and slightly upward) and a completely internal pectoral arch. In *B. linguidens* the dorsal fin originates behind the ventral fins, and the pectoral fin is very long, much longer than the ventral fin.

Fig. 22. *Benthalbella linguidens*

Natural history notes. — *Benthalbella linguidens* apparently is confined to the north Pacific, ranging from off southern California northward across the Pacific to Japan. Pearleyes usually live 1,000 feet or more beneath the surface, but move upward in the water at night, sometimes to relatively shallow depths.

They are believed to be rapid swimmers, skillful at avoiding nets, which would account for the scarcity of large adults in research collections. Some members of the family are believed to attain lengths of a foot or more, but 5 inches is the current record for *B. linguidens.* It is very difficult to interpret annual growth on the fairly large, flat otoliths of pearleyes, but three winter rings are suggested on those from a 5-inch specimen, the largest of several sets examined. Juveniles feed heavily upon crustaceans, but the stomach contents of adults usually consist almost entirely of other fishes. An adult pearleye is sometimes found in the stomach of some large, deep-feeding predatory species (lancetfish, opah, albacore, salmon, etc.). No data are available on other phases of their life history.

Fishery information. — *B. linguidens* is not abundant in any collection of deep-sea fishes, but it and other pearleyes are usually taken with fine-mesh midwater trawls. Larvae are most often captured in plankton nets.

Other family members. — Four other pearleyes belonging to two genera are known from our area (*B. dentata, B. infans, Scopelarchus analis* and *S. nicholsi*). A fifth pearleye, *S. guentheri,* may eventually show up in our fauna, for it has been found both to the south and well offshore from California. In *Scopelarchus* the dorsal fin originates anterior to the ventral fins (posterior to the ventrals in *Benthalbella*). In *S. nicholsi* the ventral fins are longer than the pectorals; in *S. analis* they are shorter. *Benthalbella dentata* can be distinguished from *B. linguidens* and *B. infans* by its 6 to 7 dorsal rays (8 to 10 in *linguidens* and *infans*), and a pectoral fin only half as long as the ventrals (pectorals of *linguidens* are as long as

the ventrals; in *infans* the pectorals are much longer).
The 27 to 29 anal rays of *B. linguidens* distinguish it
from both *B. dentata* (with 17 to 21) and *B. infans*
(with 22).

Meaning of name. — *Benthalbella* (literally, a hand-
some fish from the depths of the sea) *linguidens*
(tongue tooth, for the distinctive teeth on its tongue).

SCOPELOSAURIDAE (PAPERBONE FAMILY)
Scaly Paperbone
Scopelosaurus harryi (Mead)

Distinguishing characters. — The general body shape
(elongate, nearly round in cross section), fin sizes
and placement, large eye, and large mouth are sufficient to distinguish members of this genus. The
scaled body (in all but larval specimens) and maxillary (upper jaw) which extends to the back edge of
the eye separate the scaly paperbone from its relatives in our waters.

Fig. 23. *Scopelosaurus harryi*

Natural history notes. — *Scopelosaurus harryi* is
very rare (only six specimens known); so its distribution is probably not well defined. It has been captured
twice off southern California, twice off British Columbia, and off northern Japan. One of the British Columbia specimens at 8½ inches is the largest of the six.
The otoliths of a 6-inch specimen had four rather
vague winter rings, but since only the one set of otoliths was available, the reliability of these structures
for determining age cannot be depended upon. We
assume (from the size of the mouth) that small fishes
would form part of the diet of adult paperbones, with
crustaceans most important at younger stages, but

this is only an assumption since most of the stomachs we have examined were empty. We have no information on spawning habits, growth rates, or other phases of life history.

Fishery information — The six known specimens of *S. harryi* were captured by scientific expeditions using midwater trawls and fishing 300 feet or more beneath the surface. Large individuals apparently live in deeper water than small ones.

Other family members. — One other member of the family is known from our coast, but its identification to species is uncertain. This fish, which is sometimes regurgitated by albacore, looks generally similar to *S. harryi* but lacks scales and has a shorter maxillary. Freshly caught individuals are a beautiful, almost iridescent gold color, and have a red bar on the tail.

Meaning of name. — *Scopelosaurus* (a combination of two generic names, *Scopelus*, a lanternfish, and *Saurus*, a lizardfish, because of its presumed intermediate relationship to these two) *harryi* (for Robert R. Harry, now R. R. Rofen, who pioneered investigations of related deep-sea fishes).

NETTASTOMATIDAE (WITCH-EEL FAMILY)
Dogface Witch-eel
Facciolella gilbertii (Garman)

Distinguishing characters. — Among the eels known from our waters, the dogface witch-eel is characterized by a rather elongate snout with a blunt soft tip, a somewhat compressed whiplike tail, and several distinctive and specialized skeletal arrangements. The lack of pectoral and ventral fins and the placement of the dorsal and anal fins are also helpful in its identification.

Natural history notes. — *Facciolella gilbertii* ranges from off Point Conception to Panama (at least), and offshore for several hundred miles. Adults, and possibly the leptocephali also, inhabit scattering layers to depths of several thousand feet, but they are not captured in great abundance. Their seeming rarity may reflect a greater ability to escape capture than

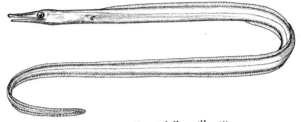

Fig. 24. *Facciolella gilbertii*

some of the other bathypelagic eels, but most likely they are minor constituents of their habitat. The largest individual we know of, a 24-incher, weighed but a few grams. The otoliths of an 18-inch individual had six winter zones, and there was an indication that this fish had first spawned during its fourth year. They are known to eat small, deep-sea crustaceans, but too few stomachs have been examined to provide more complete information about their food habits. Nothing is known about other phases of their life history.

Fishery information. — To our knowledge, *F. gilbertii* has been captured mostly in midwater and bottom trawls operated from research vessels, primarily south of California. One individual was found dead on a rocky beach where it had been cast by the waves during a previous high tide.

Other family members. — Two other members of the family, *Venefica procera* and *V. tentaculata*, are known off our coast. *Venefica* differs from *Facciolella* in having a fleshy tentacle at the tip of the snout, and in the placement of the nostrils: the posterior nostril is above and in front of the eye (in *Facciolella* the posterior nostril is slitlike and opens into the upper lip below the eye). In *V. procera* the anal fin is inserted under the 73d dorsal ray; in *V. tentaculata* it is more than 20 rays farther back.

Meaning of name. — *Facciolella* (for Luigi Facciola, an Italian ichthyologist) *gilbertii* (for Charles H. Gilbert, 1859-1928, a distinguished American ichthyologist).

CONGRIDAE (CONGER FAMILY)
Catalina Conger
Gnathophis catalinensis (Wade)

Distinguishing characters. — The eel-like body, the presence of pectoral fins, the continuous fin around the posterior tip of the body, and the placement of the posterior nostril in front of the eye distinguish the Catalina conger from all other fishes in our waters.

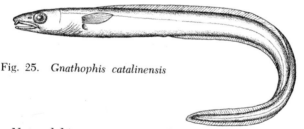

Fig. 25.   *Gnathophis catalinensis*

Natural history notes. — The range of *Gnathophis catalinensis* is undoubtedly much more extensive than has been recorded (Santa Rosa Island to San Clemente Island, California), but the secretive habits of congers and the lack of a fishery to catch them regularly may account for their rarity. The largest known individual appears to be a 16½ incher that was killed by explosives off Santa Rosa Island in 1949. This fish was not weighed. Spawning is presumed to occur in spring, but this has not been confirmed. Nothing is known of the food habits of congers, but the first individual known to science was caught on a baited hook in 30 feet of water. Skindivers report that the Catalina conger burrows rapidly, tail first, into loose sand, and appears to be fairly resistant to chemical preparations used for collecting fish. Bottom-feeding predators (e.g., rockfishes) devour conger eels when they encounter them in the open.

Fossil otoliths of extinct species have been found in Miocene deposits near Bakersfield, California; so the family is an ancient one in our waters.

Fishery information. — Of the few Catalina congers known, one was caught on a baited hook, two were caught in purse seines that dragged the bottom during retrieval, two were killed by explosives, one was found in a rockfish stomach, and two small ones were picked up by divers using fish-collecting chemicals in 100 feet of water. Larvae may have been caught in plankton nets and midwater trawls, but none has been identified.

Other family members. — One other congrid, *Xenomystax atrarius*, has been taken off California. It differs from *G. catalinensis* in having an elongate snout with the posterior nostril about halfway between the tip of the snout and the eye. Specimens of *Ariosoma gilberti* and *Uroconger varidens* were captured just south of our area; these congrids may eventually show up in our fauna.

Meaning of name. — *Gnathophis* (jaw snake, in allusion to the snakelike jaw) *catalinensis* (belonging to Catalina, site of the first capture).

OPHICHTHIDAE (SNAKE-EEL FAMILY)
Yellow Snake-eel
Ophichthus zophochir (Jordan and Gilbert)

Distinguishing characters. — The stiff, pointed tail of the yellow snake-eel, which is never adorned with either a dorsal or an anal fin, and the plain, unspotted body distinguish it from all other California eels.

[57]

Natural history notes. — *Ophichthus zophochir* ranges from San Francisco to Panama, but is not abundant north of central Baja California. Larval eels, probably including members of this family, often

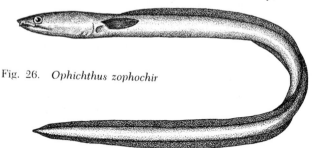

Fig. 26. *Ophichthus zophochir*

are important constituents of fish catches made with midwater trawls, sometimes hundreds of miles offshore. Few of these transparent eel larvae, better known as leptocephali, have ever been identified with the adult stage into which they eventually transform. Although leptocephali of *O. zophochir* may be a part of the bathypelagic community, the adults typically inhabit shallow inshore areas, including the intertidal. If they are startled or disturbed while moving about in the open they burrow rapidly into the bottom, tail first, but once beneath the sand they often reverse direction and travel head first.

The largest of several dozen observed during the last two decades was just under 30 inches long and one pound in weight. The otoliths of several 22- to 28-inch adults had from six to nine winter zones, indicating a maximum age in excess of ten years. Females captured during late summer appeared to be nearing the onset of spawning. Both clam and fish remains have been found in snake-eel stomachs.

Fishery information. — Eel leptocephali have been caught at the surface with a dipnet, usually at night after they had been attracted to the side of a drifting ship by a powerful electric light, but most larval specimens have been taken with midwater trawling gear, and in plankton nets and predator stomachs. Adult yellow snake-eels usually are caught on hook and line, but they are easily captured by hand and in shrimp trawls. In tropical areas, skindivers often observe snake-eels moving about near the bottom, especially in the late afternoon.

Other family members. — Two of the three other snake-eels known to California (*Ophichthus triserialis* and *Myrichthys tigrinus*) are covered with small to large round blackish spots. *Ophichthus triserialis* has a well-developed pectoral fin, sharp teeth, and a dorsal fin that originates posterior to the gill opening, whereas *M. tigrinus* has a rudimentary pectoral fin, conical, blunt, or molar-like teeth, and a dorsal that commences in advance of the gill opening. "*Hesperomyrus fryi*," the only other member of the family in our waters, resembles *O. zophochir* in being plain-colored, but differs in that both the dorsal and anal fins continue over the surface of the tail, which is not sharply pointed.

Meaning of name. — *Ophichthus* (snake fish) *zophochir* (dark hand, in allusion to the dusky pectoral fin).

DERICHTHYIDAE (NECK EEL FAMILY)
Neck Eel
Derichthys serpentinus Gill

Distinguishing characters. — The neck eel is the only eel in our waters with a short, rounded snout, a constricted neck region, a dorsal fin that commences well behind the pectorals, and an anal fin that originates posterior to midbody. The numerous large pores on the head (around the eyes and along the lower jaw) and the nearly horizontal gill slit below and in front of the pectorals are additional helpful characters.

Natural history notes. — *Derichthys serpentinus* is found in warm and temperate seas throughout the world. In the eastern Pacific it ranges from off south-

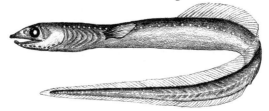

Fig. 27. *Derichthys serpentinus*

ern California to Chile (33° S.), but is not found abundantly anywhere within this range. Most captures have been made at depths exceeding 1,500 feet, but shallower than 6,000 feet. The largest individual noted seems to be a 10½-incher caught in the Atlantic. The tiny otoliths of a 7-inch "adult" from our waters had three winter growth zones; so the species apparently does not attain an extreme old age. Based upon research conducted on several Bermudan specimens, *D. serpentinus* transforms from a leptocephalus when about 2 inches long. The ovaries of a ripe female contained nearly 4,100 eggs, each of which was 0.75 of a millimeter (about 1/35th of an inch) in diameter. A similar number of smaller eggs was also present, indicating more than one spawning per season. Crustaceans comprised most of the food items noted in their stomachs.

Fishery information. — Midwater trawls and similar nets seem to be the only successful gear for capturing these eels, but they are never found in abundance; one or two individuals during a month-long trawling cruise (in areas and depths where they are known to occur) is about par.

Other family members. — *D. serpentinus* is the only member of the family known.

Meaning of name. — *Derichthys* (neck fish, alluding to the constricted neck) *serpentinus* (snakelike).

SERRIVOMERIDAE (SAWTOOTH SNIPE-EEL FAMILY)

Sawtooth Snipe-eel
Serrivomer sector Garman

Distinguishing characters. — The eel-like body, elongate jaws, saw-edged vomerine plate in the midline of the roof of the mouth, and the insertion of the dorsal fin at least one head length behind the gill opening distinguish the sawtooth snipe-eel from all other fishes in our waters.

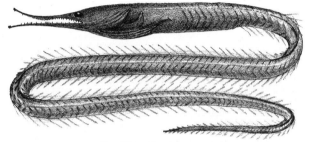

Fig. 28. *Serrivomer sector*

Natural history notes. — *Serrivomer sector* ranges throughout most of the temperate and tropic eastern Pacific Ocean, from somewhere north of San Francisco to northern Chile (28° S.) and offshore for a considerable distance. At maximum size, possibly 30 inches, this snipe-eel weighs slightly less than a pound. An examination of numerous otoliths revealed as many as nine winter zones, with an indication that spawning occurs first in the fourth year. In our area spawning takes place mostly in spring and early summer. These eels feed primarily upon crustaceans, and to a lesser extent upon small cephalopods and fishes. They probably are captured and eaten by large predatory fishes, but we have no reports of their occurrence in the stomachs of any of these.

Fishery information. — To the best of our knowledge, *S. sector* has been captured only with midwater trawls, usually at depths below 1,000 feet, but at night some individuals have been taken near the surface, apparently having migrated there after sunset.

Other family members. — No other member of the family is known within several thousand miles of California.

Meaning of name. — *Serrivomer* (serrate vomer) *sector* (apparently alluding to the manner in which the platelike vomer divides the roof of the mouth into equal parts).

NEMICHTHYIDAE (THREADTAIL SNIPE-EEL FAMILY)

Slender Snipe-eel
Nemichthys scolopaceus Richardson

Distinguishing characters. — The slender eel-like body, the excessively attenuate jaws which diverge toward the tips as the upper jaw curves upward, the threadlike tail, and the vent in the vicinity of the throat distinguish the slender snipe-eel from all other marine fishes in our waters.

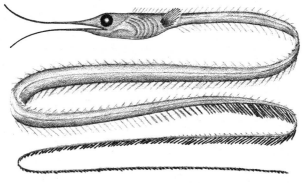

Fig. 29. *Nemichthys scolopaceus*

Natural history notes. — *Nemichthys scolopaceus* is found in all world seas: Atlantic, Pacific, and Indian oceans, Mediterranean Sea, and others. In the north

Pacific, slender snipe-eels have been taken all the way from the equator to Alaska and across to Japan. They are usually captured at depths exceeding 1,000 feet, but occasional individuals are found in waters where the bottom is less than 300 feet down. Snipe-eel larvae (leptocephali) are transparent, shaped like an elongate leaf that tapers at both ends. These leptocephali shrink slightly and take on adult form when they are about 8 inches long.

The largest known adult seems to be a 57-incher caught in the western Atlantic. A snipe-eel of that size weighs only a few ounces at most. The otoliths from several individuals 30 to 40 inches long were dense, and indications of growth were obscure, but ages of five to six years were discernible, leading us to believe that maximum ages would exceed ten years. Spawning habits are not known.

Although the only food items we have found in their stomachs have been shrimplike crustaceans, *Nemichthys* should be capable of catching and eating small fishes and cephalopods also.

Predatory fishes often feed upon eel larvae and some of these unquestionably are *Nemichthys*. A 30-inch snipe-eel was spit up by a rockfish trawled in 130 fathoms near Anacapa Island; so other large fishes probably prey upon them also.

The skeletal imprint of a threadtail snipe-eel was found on a slab of Miocene diatomite from southern California; we do not know whether it represents *Nemichthys* or *Avocettina*.

Fishery information. — Most snipe-eels are caught from research vessels using midwater trawls, but one 30-inch fish was caught by a commercial fisherman at or near the surface in a nighttime purse-seine set, and an individual of similar size was spit up by a rockfish. In other areas occasional specimens have been cast ashore during stormy periods and left stranded by receding tides.

Other family members. — *Avocettina gilli* and *A. infans* are the only other snipe-eels in our area. They differ from *Nemichthys* in having the vent fairly well back on the body, and in having only one set of pores along the lateral line compared with five in *Nemichthys*. *A. gilli* has fewer than 280 rays in its dorsal fin, whereas *A. infans* has more than 320.

Meaning of name. — *Nemichthys* (thread fish) *scolopaceus* (snipe) — a threadlike fish with a snipelike "bill."

CYEMIDAE (BOBTAIL SNIPE-EEL FAMILY)
Bobtail Snipe-eel
Cyema atrum Günther

Distinguishing characters. — The eel-like body, the elongate jaws, the dorsal fin originating above the anal fin about halfway back on the body, and the dart-like profile these fins present in terminating distinguish the bobtail snipe-eel from all other fishes in our waters.

Fig. 30. *Cyema atrum*

Natural history notes. — *Cyema atrum* is worldwide in distribution, ranging in the eastern Pacific from off Tillamook Head, Oregon, to Panama, at least. One of our smallest eels, it seldom if ever exceeds 6 inches in length or about half an ounce in weight. The semitransparent, deep-bodied, leaflike leptocephalus metamorphoses when it is about 3 inches long, and is believed to move deeper in the water at that time. An examination of several sets of *Cyema* otoliths failed to reveal any valid information regarding age, although some of the larger individuals might have been two or three years old. In our waters, spawning probably takes place mostly in spring and early summer, but again factual information is scanty. Small crustaceans prevailed in the few stomachs we examined.

Fishery information. — The only captures of *C. atrum* that we could verify were made with midwater trawling gear, usually at relatively great depths — 2,000 feet and deeper. We feel certain that they are preyed upon by larger fishes living at these depths, but have not found their remains in any stomachs we have examined, and do not know of such occurrences elsewhere.

Other family members. — No other family members have been reported.

Meaning of name. — *Cyema* (embryo, possibly in reference to its "unfinished" appearance) *atrum* (black).

SACCOPHARYNGIDAE (WHIPTAIL GULPER FAMILY)

Whiptail Gulper
Saccopharynx sp.

Distinguishing characters. — Because of their large mouth, lack of opercular bones and ventral fins, blackish color, and distinctively shaped body, members of this family can be confused only with umbrellamouth gulpers. However, they are easily distinguished from *Eurypharynx* by the presence of teeth in the jaws, the

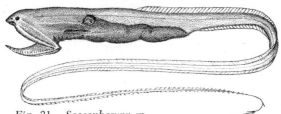

Fig. 31. *Saccopharynx* sp.

origin of the dorsal fin far behind the head, the luminous grooves (appearing as white lines) that originate on the head and extend on each side of the back and dorsal fin to near the end of the tail, and the gill opening that is nearer the tip of the snout than the anus.

Natural history notes. — Specimens of *Saccopharynx* have been captured in the eastern Pacific between southern California and Panama Bay, at least. The whiptail gulper has a leptocephalus-like larval stage, but even these are seldom taken alive within 5,000 feet of the surface. Adults generally inhabit even greater depths. Some members of the family are known to reach a length of nearly 6 feet, but those off our coast seldom exceed one-third of the reported maximum. The tiny otoliths from a 15-inch fish netted off our coast had five very distinct winter rings, and those from a smaller individual had three, but we have no idea of the maximum age (or size) attained by the species inhabiting our waters. A very complex luminous organ near the tip of the tail may function as a lure for attracting food, but this is pure speculation. The only food items found in their stomachs have been fishes, usually quite large. Other phases of life history are unknown.

Fishery information. — Most members of the family have been captured with midwater trawls being fished at great depths. In the Atlantic some of the largest individuals were found floating dead at the surface, possibly because they rose too rapidly from the depths in pursuit of prey, and expanding gases in their system kept them from returning; but exact information is lacking.

Other family members. — Fewer than twenty-five whiptail gulpers have been captured or noted from all world seas. These have generally been assigned to four species in the single genus *Saccopharynx*. Unfortunately, because so few members of the family are known, the exact status of the various species has not been satisfactorily worked out. Only one species is known in the eastern Pacific Ocean, but its specific assignment must await further comparison and study.

Meaning of name. — *Saccopharynx* (sack pharynx, for the greatly distensible throat).

EURYPHARYNGIDAE (UMBRELLAMOUTH GULPER FAMILY)
Umbrellamouth Gulper
Eurypharynx pelecanoides Vaillant

Distinguishing characters. — Because of its enormous mouth, distensible gut, and long tapering tail, this black, scaleless, bathypelagic fish is difficult to mistake. The dorsal fin originating on the head, gill opening nearer the anus than the tip of the snout, and lack of teeth in the jaws will clinch the identification of the umbrellamouth gulper.

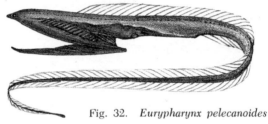

Fig. 32. *Eurypharynx pelecanoides*

Natural history notes. — *Eurypharynx pelecanoides* is known throughout the world, but only in tropic and temperate seas. In the eastern Pacific a few individuals have been captured between southern California and Peru, usually at great depths — 4,000 to 10,000 feet or deeper. The species is said to attain a length of 24 to 30 inches, but those from our waters have been shorter than 16 inches. The tiny otoliths of several 10- to 15-inch individuals were examined, but no evidence of age was discernible. A small luminous organ at the tip of the tail is believed to be useful in attracting food items, but because of its placement (as far from the mouth as possible), the fish would have to be swimming in tight circles or some other odd pattern for the "lure" to be useful. Umbrellamouth gulpers have a leptocephalus-like larval stage;

[67]

because of this, the family is often likened to the eels, but its exact relationship is not completely understood. The only food items found in umbrellamouth gulper stomachs have been fishes, some almost as large as the gulper that swallowed them.

Fishery information. — Although *E. pelecanoides* is known from tropic and temperate seas throughout the world, fewer than 300 individuals have been captured (including larvae). Perhaps a dozen specimens have been taken off our coast, all in midwater trawls and at great depths.

Other family members. — No other member of the family is known.

Meaning of name. — *Eurypharynx* (wide or broad pharynx) *pelecanoides* (in allusion to the pelican-like mouth and throat).

CETOMIMIDAE (FLABBY WHALEFISH FAMILY)

Pacific Whalefish
Cetomimus sp.

Distinguishing characters. — Pacific whalefishes are aberrant deep-sea forms marked by darkly pigmented, soft, flabby bodies. They may be distinguished from others by the long lower jaw, reaching almost to the operculum, well-developed eyes, granular-like teeth on the jaws, a network of luminous tissue around the anus and alongside the anal and dorsal fins, and dorsal and anal fins containing fewer than 20 rays each.

Fig. 33. *Cetomimus* sp.

The luminous tissue does not form discrete organs, as

in the lanternfishes, but is soft, mushy, and fleshlike; it probably glows reddish-orange in life. Only whip-tail gulpers (*Saccopharynx*) are known to have luminous tissue similar to that of the whalefishes. In these fishes the tissue lies in two parallel troughs along the back, and reportedly glows red in life. The Pacific whalefish has a hollow tubelike lateral line with large obvious pores, smooth skin, and no ventral fins.

Natural history notes. — *Cetomimus* ranges from off southern California south to the Gulf of California, but since it is known from fewer than ten individuals this probably does not represent its entire habitat. At first sight one imagines a very tiny whale, owing to the black globular shape and great gaping mouth. It was difficult to distinguish growth zones on whalefish otoliths, but those from a 9-inch *Cetostomus regani* (a close relative of *Cetomimus*) had more than three winter rings, but fewer than five. Very little is known of the life habits and vertical distribution of these fishes; however, those from off California had fed upon small crustaceans.

Fishery information. — Whalefishes are taken only with deep-sea trawling gear in oceanic waters. Information regarding specific depth of capture is lacking, but none has been taken in our area in waters shallower than 2,500 feet.

Other family members. — Four genera are currently recognized within the family: *Ditropichthys*, *Cetomimus*, *Cetostomus*, and *Gyrinomimus*. All but *Gyrinomimus* have been recorded from the California fauna. *Cetostomus*, like *Cetomimus*, has a very long lower jaw and well-developed eyes, but differs from *Cetomimus* (and *Ditropichthys*) in having more than 30 rays in the dorsal and anal fins. *Ditropichthys* has a short lower jaw, which ends about halfway between the snout and the opercular margin; it also has tiny degenerate eyes.

Meaning of name. — *Cetomimus* (an imitator of a whale, in reference to the basic body plan).

RONDELETIIDAE (REDMOUTH WHALEFISH FAMILY)

Redmouth Whalefish
Rondeletia loricata Abe and Hotta

Distinguishing characters. — The rare, odd-colored redmouth whalefish is immediately recognizable by its dark brown body and reddish-orange mouth, jaws, operculum, and fin bases. It has a large box-shaped head, and a number of bony protuberances (on head and body) which are rough to the touch. The posterior part of the body is marked by a series of vertically aligned lateral-line pores.

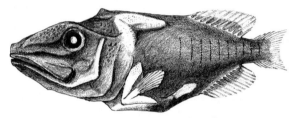

Fig. 34. *Rondeletia loricata*

Natural history notes. — *Rondeletia loricata* is very poorly known. Possibly twenty individuals have been taken from all world oceans, and these range in length from 2 to 6 inches. The otoliths of a 6-inch fish had seven quite good winter rings, indicating that it was in its eighth year when caught. Although no distinct photophores or luminescing organs as such are found, the reddish-orange outer tissue layer is believed to be luminous in life. We have no information on food habits, maturity, or spawning.

Fishery information. — *R. loricata* has been taken only with midwater trawls operated during deep-sea oceanographic expeditions; four individuals have been taken off southern California. Although data are lacking for specific depth distribution off our coast, the

[70]

redmouth whalefish is never caught in waters shallower than 2,000 feet.

Other family members. — No other member of the family is known from the Pacific Ocean.

Meaning of name. — *Rondeletia* (named for the great French ichthyologist of the sixteenth century, William Rondelet, 1507-1566), *loricata* (clad in mail, in reference to the bony protuberances around the body).

MORIDAE (CODLING FAMILY)
Flatnose Codling
Antimora rostrata (Günther)

Distinguishing characters. — The broad, depressed snout, forming a spadelike rostrum with sharp lateral edges, the inferior mouth, barbel under the tip of the lower jaw, and filamentous ray in the first dorsal fin distinguish the flatnose codling from all other fishes off our coast.

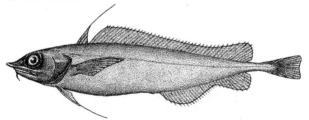

Fig. 35. *Antimora rostrata*

Natural history notes. — *Antimora rostrata* has been captured on both sides of the north Pacific Ocean, as far south as Central America on our coast. It lives on the bottom, and has been trawled in depths of 1,200 to about 10,000 feet. Most individuals we have seen were 10 to 15 inches long, but some exceed 26 inches. The otoliths are very dense, but growth zones show up well on broken cross sections, and from these it appears that the flatnose codling lives longer than ten years. No biological studies have been conducted on the species, but it is believed that the adults will eat most mollusks and crustaceans they encounter in their habitat, and possibly a few slow-moving fishes if they are small enough to fit the mouth.

Fossil otoliths of morids are abundant in Pleistocene, Pliocene, and Miocene deposits throughout southern California, and morid skeletal "imprints" are commonly encountered in Miocene diatomites and shales.

Fishery information. — Flatnose codlings are usually caught in trawl nets that are fishing on the bottom in muddy (as compared to rocky or shelly) areas. A few have been attracted to baited traps in very deep water, and they will take a baited hook if some other fish does not get there first.

Other family members. — Although two other California fishes have been placed in this family, only *Physiculus rastrelliger* rightly belongs here. *Physiculus* has 8 to 10 rays in the first dorsal fin (*Antimora* has only 4 or 5), has a terminal mouth, and an incomplete lateral line. These characters, in conjunction with its elongate, deeply notched second dorsal and anal fins, distinguish it from other marine fishes. Another codlike fish, *Melanonus zugmayeri*, has been assigned to

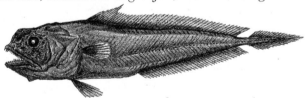

Fig. 36. *Melanonus zugmayeri*

this family by some ichthyologists, but it definitely does not belong here. Its proper family designation must await action from those who are currently studying the problem.

Meaning of name. — *Antimora* (the opposite of *Mora,* a related genus) *rostrata* (longnosed).

MACROURIDAE (RATTAIL FAMILY)
California Rattail
Nezumia stelgidolepis (Gilbert)

Distinguishing characters. — The general shape of the California rattail, its dusky over-all coloration, the single chin whisker, or barbel, at the tip of the lower jaw, the serrate and rather firmly embedded scales, the anus in a black, scaleless area nearer the pelvic fin insertions than the anal fin, and the rather broad interspace between the two dorsal fins distinguish it from all other species in our waters.

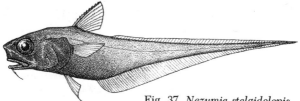

Fig. 37. *Nezumia stelgidolepis*

Natural history notes. — *Nezumia stelgidolepis* ranges from off northern California (Eureka area) at least as far south as the vicinity of Cedros Island, Baja California. One individual was caught in water as shallow as 200 to 300 feet, but most have come from depths of 1,000 to 2,000 feet or more. These rattails do not seem to grow very big; a 17½-inch fish from off Point Vicente was the largest of more than a hundred examined in recent years. The otoliths are extremely large and dense, but several sets from 12- to 15-inch fish all had three winter zones. Even if one winter zone was not seen, these fish would not have been older than four years. Very little is known regarding the various phases of life history. Food items are generally forcibly regurgitated by the fish's expanding gas bladder as it is hauled from the depths, but fish remains have been caught inside the mouth on a few individuals. They are opportunistic feeders and will eat whatever animal food they encounter in their natural habitat, so long as it is of appropriate size.

Macrourid otoliths are occasionally found in Miocene and younger deposits in California, whereas scales are abundant in Miocene and older deposits.

Fishery information. — *Nezumia* captures have been made almost exclusively with bottom-trawling gear and in traps, but at least one individual was caught on a set line. Other members of the family are occasionally found floating at the surface, but not *N. stelgidolepis.*

Other family members. — Six other species of rattails have been reported from our area, but since rattail taxonomy in the eastern Pacific is so poorly understood, there could be six or more additional species. *Coelorhynchus scaphopsis*, captured twice off Santa Barbara, has a smooth first dorsal spine to distinguish it from *Coryphaenoides* and *Nezumia*, in which this spine is serrate. In *Coryphaenoides* the anus is directly in front of the anal fin, whereas in *Nezumia* it is closer to the pelvic insertion than the anal.

Meaning of name. — *Nezumia* (from the Japanese nezumi — rat) *stelgidolepis* (scraper scale, for the rasplike scales that cover the body).

OPHIDIIDAE (CUSK-EEL FAMILY)
Spotted Cusk-eel
Otophidium taylori (Girard)

Distinguishing characters. — The spotted eel-like body and the pair of chin whiskers, or feelers (modi-

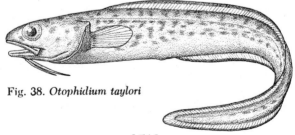

Fig. 38. *Otophidium taylori*

fied pelvic fins), near the tip of the lower jaw distinguish the spotted cusk-eel from all other fishes on our coast. Regardless of its eel-like appearance, it is not a true eel.

Natural history notes. — *Otophidium taylori* ranges from northern Oregon to San Cristobal Bay, Baja California, generally living at or near the bottom in depths of 60 to 800 feet or more. Juveniles 2 to 3 inches long apparently lead a pelagic (or bathypelagic) existence in offshore waters. Adults are believed to be primarily nocturnal, remaining hidden beneath rubble, and in crevices and holes during daylight hours. Cusk-eels are noted for the ability to swim backward, using the tail for guidance. When startled or disturbed, they often burrow rapidly into the bottom, tail first; otherwise they spend most of their time "standing" erect with the tail bent at a 90° angle along the bottom or inserted into a hole or crack.

The otoliths of a very large individual, 14¼ inches long and weighing ten ounces, had only two winter zones, but everything about this fish indicated that it was a freakishly developed "giant." Other individuals, nearly that size, appeared to have been at least six to eight years old.

Cusk-eels are known to feed upon a wide variety of small fishes, octopuses, and crustaceans. The remains of adults have been found in the stomachs of numerous predatory fishes, and a few diving birds such as the cormorant. They also seem to be a favorite food of the California sea lion. Small pelagic juveniles are seldom seen except in the stomach of an albacore or in the catch from a midwater trawl which has been towed over very deep water many miles offshore.

Fossil cusk-eel otoliths are common constituents of marine Pliocene and Pleistocene deposits throughout California.

Fishery information. — *O. taylori* is most often seen in fish and shrimp catches made with bottom-trawling gear, but occasional specimens are caught on hook and line or in fish, octopus, and shrimp traps, are speared by skindivers, or are found in the stomachs of rockfish, yellowtail, albacore, and similar predatory species. Many cusk-eels are caught incidentally with other species in purse seines and bait nets.

Other family members. — One other cusk-eel is known from our area, the plain-colored *O. scrippsi*, which lives in shallower water and ranges farther south than *O. taylori*.

Meaning of name. — *Otophidium* (ear, pertaining to the large saccular otolith or ear stone) *taylori* (for A. S. Taylor, its discoverer).

BROTULIDAE (BROTULA FAMILY)
Paperbone Brotula
Lamprogrammus niger Alcock

Distinguishing characters. — The crested head with its papery bony structure, long-based dorsal and anal fins joined to the caudal, absence of ventral fins, large lateral line scales, and luminous patches and spots on the head and body distinguish the paperbone brotula from all other marine fishes.

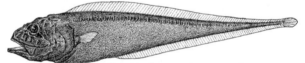

Fig. 39. *Lamprogrammus niger*

Natural history notes. — *Lamprogrammus niger* has been captured in most of the temperate and subtropical seas of the world, but is not abundantly taken anywhere, including off California. Although it has been considered a brotulid because of "structural similarities," it seems to us that it is more dissimilar than similar to the typical brotulid, if such there be. In many brotulids, copulation takes place and fertilization is internal (this does not appear to be true of *Lamprogrammus*). Other peculiar characteristics include the lack of ventral fins, the presence of luminous organs, and some very unbrotulid-like otoliths. The otoliths offer no clues to the age attained by *Lamprogrammus*. We have no information on food, reproductive habits, or behavior of the paperbone brotula, but believe that it feeds primarily upon an assortment of small crustaceans.

Brotulid otoliths (not those of *Lamprogrammus*) have been found in several southern California fossil deposits.

Fishery information. — To our knowledge, *L. niger* has been caught only with midwater trawls and similar gear operated from research vessels.

Other family members. — The four other brotulids known from our waters are easy to distinguish. The lower pectoral rays of *Dicrolene* are free and elongate. Among the three with normal pectoral fins, *Brosmophycis* has a caudal fin that is distinct and separate from the dorsal and anal fins. In *Cataetyx* and *Oli-*

Fig. 40. *Dicrolene* sp.

gopus the dorsal and anal fins are continuous with the caudal, but *Oligopus* has two overlapping lateral lines, whereas *Cataetyx* has only one.

Meaning of name. — *Lamprogrammus* (shining line, in allusion to the luminous lateral line) *niger* (black, the body color).

ZOARCIDAE (EELPOUT FAMILY)
Twoline Eelpout
Bothrocara brunneum (Bean)

Distinguishing characters. — The twoline eelpout is the only eelpout with two lateral lines, a terminal mouth, a snout with a flat or concave lateral profile, and gill rakers that are short and blunt-ended.

Natural history notes. — Bothrocara brunneum ranges from the Bering Sea to the vicinity of San Francisco. It lives on the bottom where sandy muds

Fig. 41. *Bothrocara brunneum*

or muds prevail, and is seldom captured in waters shallower than 2,000 feet or deeper than 6,000 feet. It attains a length of at least 2 feet and a weight in excess of two pounds. The otoliths are very dense and do not indicate age, although special techniques might reveal such data. The stomach contents of several individuals indicate that *B. brunneum* feeds upon a wide variety of bottom-dwelling organisms, probably eating anything it encounters that has food value and is small enough to ingest. No information is available on age, growth rates, spawning activities, or other vital statistics.

Zoarcid otoliths, although not those of *Bothrocara*, have been found in several southern California Pliocene and Pleistocene deposits.

Fishery information. — B. brunneum is captured exclusively with trawling gear that is towed along the floor of the sea. Commercial fishermen seldom net more than one or two individuals per hour of trawling, and virtually never catch any in waters shallower than 1,500 feet.

Other family members. — At least seventeen other eelpouts inhabit the waters off our coast, but many are poorly known. Members of four genera (*Bothrocara, Lycodapus, Maynea, Melanostigma*) lack pelvic fins, whereas pelvics are present in *Aprodon, Embryx, Lycodes, Lycodopsis,* and *Lyconema.* Numerous other characters, including gill membrane articulation, finray counts, dentition, skin texture, presence or absence of barbels, head and body scalation, body shape and depth, are used to distinguish various genera and species within these two basic groups of zoarcids. Sexual dimorphism (i.e., females of some species having different dentition than males, etc.) causes some confusion in zoarcid taxonomy.

Meaning of name. — *Bothrocara* (cavity head, for the pitted appearance of the head owing to sensory pores) *brunneum* (brown, the body color).

MACRORHAMPHOSIDAE (SNIPEFISH FAMILY)
Slender Snipefish
Macrorhamphosus gracilis (Lowe)

Distinguishing characters. — The combination of a short, high spinous dorsal fin, ventral fins that are nearer the tip of the tail than the snout, a laterally compressed body, and a tubular snout distinguishes the slender snipefish from all other marine fishes in our area.

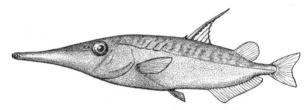

Fig. 42. *Macrorhamphosus gracilis*

Natural history notes. — Although *Macrorhamphosus gracilis* was reported from Santa Catalina Island in 1920, the species apparently was not taken off California again until November, 1962, when one was disgorged by a rockfish that was caught in 600 to 700 feet of water outside Santa Monica Bay. Possibly 500 others of these small fishes were captured off Baja California, south to about Magdalena Bay, during this forty-year period, but until 1967 their occurrence off California was unusual. Late in January, 1967, two small individuals were picked up on a rocky beach at Santa Catalina Island, and throughout February and March reports were received that small schools of snipefishes (perhaps 50 to 100 individuals) were scattered over wide areas on the inshore sides of Santa Catalina and San Clemente islands. During these three months about 20 live individuals were salvaged from the bait well of a sportfishing boat at Ensenada. They were transported to the aquarium at Scripps Institution of Oceanography, where most of them survived and began flourishing on a diet of brine shrimp. This "invasion" of snipefishes culminated on the night of April 26-27, when two purse seiners fishing at Pyramid Cove, San Clemente Island, set their nets on what they believed were schools of Pacific mackerel, but which were actually large schools of *M. gracilis.* Fortunately they were using fine-meshed anchovy nets or the schools would have escaped completely. Possibly 2,000 snipefishes were retained and more than 600 of these were in good enough condition to preserve for posterity. At 12 snipefishes per ounce, these two schools, containing an estimated 40 to 45 tons according to the fishermen, would have yielded at least 15 million individuals. In view of the fact that probably fewer than 1,000 *M. gracilis* were known from all the seas of the world prior to this occurrence, their appearance in large, dense schools makes one wonder about other fish species that are believed to be rare.

Most of the snipefishes seen in the eastern Pacific have been only 2 or 3 inches long, but two specimens, one from a yellowtail stomach and the other from the Santa Monica Bay rockfish, exceeded 4 inches. The largest of these, at 4¼ inches, is about 2 inches short of the known maximum size for the species. The tiny otoliths of the 4¼-inch individual from Santa Monica Bay had five excellent winter zones and an opaque margin, indicating that this fish was in its sixth year.

In our waters, snipefish ovaries are just commencing

to develop in April; a 3-inch female spit up by an albacore in September contained eggs that seemed to be mature, indicating fall spawning for the species. The tiny terminal mouth at the end of a long snout and some of the crustacean remains found in their stomachs lead us to believe that snipefishes feed at or near the bottom during much of their lifetime.

Fishery information. — Most of the 500 or so snipefish known from the eastern north Pacific before 1967 were dipnetted at the surface after they had been attracted to a powerful light hung over the side of an anchored or drifting vessel during nighttime hours. Most of the others were regurgitated by various predatory species including albacore, yellowtail, and rockfish. The rockfish almost certainly caught the snipefish it ate either at or near the bottom.

Other family members. — No other member of the family is known from within several thousand miles of California.

Meaning of name. — *Macrorhamphosus* (long snout) *gracilis* (slender).

OREOSOMATIDAE (OREO FAMILY)
Oxeye Oreo
Allocyttus folletti Myers

Distinguishing characters. — The combination of a very large eye, a protractile mouth, and a compressed but quite deep (perchlike) body distinguishes the oxeye oreo. The dusky coloration, dorsal and anal fins containing 30 to 33 soft rays each, and tenaciously adherent ctenoid scales of the nape, breast, belly, and along the bases of the dorsal and anal fins (scales on midsides are cycloid and deciduous) are additional useful characters.

Natural history notes. — Fewer than a dozen specimens of *Allocyttus folletti* are known to science, and all were captured off central and northern California, between Gorda Point and Crescent City. The first, a 15-incher, trawled in 230 fathoms off the Eel River in 1949, is the largest. No information is available on its life history, except age, and that may not be accurate. The otoliths of an 11-inch fish weighing slightly

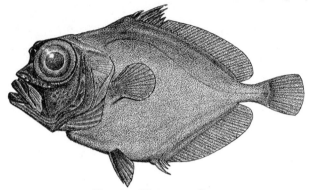

Fig. 43. *Allocyttus folletti*

more than a pound had three quite good winter zones, indicating an age of just over three years, but otoliths of eight other individuals were of no use for determining age; so the accuracy of the reading from the one good pair is in doubt.

Fishery information. — All the oxeye oreos known to date have been captured in otter trawls being fished by commercial fishermen in depths exceeding 1,200 feet (200 fathoms).

Other family members. — A single individual of a close relative, *A. verrucosus,* was caught in surface gill nets several hundred miles off the coast of British Columbia in 1956 (50° N., 150° W.). It can be distinguished from *A. folletti* by the two rows of enlarged scutes on the sides of the body, between the pectoral and pelvic fins.

Meaning of name. — *Allocyttus* (a different *Cyttus*) *folletti* (for W. I. Follett, well-known ichthyologist associated with the California Academy of Sciences).

ZEIDAE (DORY FAMILY)
Mirror Dory
Zenopsis nebulosa (Temminck and Schlegel)

Distinguishing characters. — The general shape of the mirror dory, the protrusible mouth, and the scaleless body (except for the rows of large bony shields or bucklers on each side of the base of the dorsal and anal fins, and in the throat and chest region) distinguish it from all other fishes found off our coast.

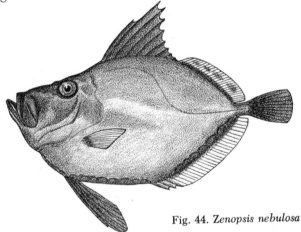

Fig. 44. *Zenopsis nebulosa*

Natural history notes. — *Zenopsis nebulosa* is known in the eastern Pacific from only three individuals, one from off Santa Cruz, one from Point Sal and the third from off Ventura. In other parts of the world it is found both north and south of the equator, but is seldom caught in quantity. Little information is available on maximum sizes, weights, ages, or other vital statistics. The largest of the three from our coast was 19 inches long; it was not weighed, but probably did not exceed 3½ or 4 pounds. The otoliths of this fish, a mature female, had seven winter zones. Its stomach contained the remains of a 4-inch rockfish.

Fishery information. — The three individuals caught in our waters were taken with otter trawls being fished along the bottom in 80 to 120 fathoms. Elsewhere they are usually caught with bottom trawling gear in "deep water" (presumed to mean 1,000 feet or deeper), but some catches have been made in gill nets within 150 feet of the surface. One setting of a gill net off Japan (to a depth of about 100 feet) yielded 22 mirror dories. We are informed that *Zenopsis* is fished commercially in New Zealand waters by otter trawling.

Other family members. — No other family member is known within several thousand miles of California. The closest relative may possibly be in Hawaiian waters.

Meaning of name. — *Zenopsis* (*Zeus*-like, *Zeus* being a genus of dories common to the Atlantic and Mediterranean) *nebulosa* (dark or clouded) — a dark *Zeus*-like fish.

LAMPRIDAE (OPAH FAMILY)
Opah
Lampris regius (Bonnaterre)

Distinguishing characters. — The iridescent, disk-shaped body with white spots and crimson fins distinguishes the opah (sometimes called moonfish) from other fish.

Natural history notes. — In the eastern Pacific, specimens of *Lampris regius* have been caught far north in Alaska and near Cape San Lucas, Baja California, and at many intermediate localities. Offshore they range across the Pacific, and are also found in the Atlantic Ocean, both north and south of the equator. Although opahs have been reported to attain weights of 500 to 600 pounds and lengths of 6 feet, we have not found any authentic record of a weight of even 200 pounds. The heaviest of several hundred individuals from our coast weighed 160 pounds and was 4½ feet long.

Opahs apparently will eat whatever food is available in their area, and often in great quantities. The stomach of a 126-pounder caught near Anacapa Island

Fig. 45. *Lampris regius*

in 1959 contained the remains of 63 fishes (51 hake, 4 rockfish, 1 brotulid, and 7 unidentifiables), 8 cephalopods, and 7 pelagic crabs. Another opah, caught on longline gear several hundred miles offshore, had eaten 5 lancetfish, each 3 to 4 feet long.

We have no information on ages, spawning habits, or migrations, although a large female caught in the early spring appeared to be nearly ready to spawn.

Fishery information. — During albacore season each year a few fishermen catch opahs off California, especially in the seas between the northern Channel Islands (Anacapa, Santa Cruz, Santa Rosa, and San Miguel) and the Coronado Islands. Some of these fish are hooked near the surface and some quite deep, some on live bait and some on trolled artificial lures. Opahs are taken in fair abundance in tuna longline fisheries conducted on the high seas. These longline-caught fish are usually hooked 400 to 1,000 feet beneath the surface. Occasionally an opah becomes entangled in a gill net which has been set for other species. The salmon-colored flesh of the opah is quite tasty, but rather dry when cooked; it is best when smoked.

Other family members. — *Lampris regius* is the only living member of the family known at present, although several other scientific names have been applied to opahs throughout the world. A Miocene fossil opah found near El Capitan (Santa Barbara County) was named *Lampris zatima.*

Meaning of name. — *Lampris* (brilliant) *regius* (king).

LOPHOTIDAE (CRESTFISH FAMILY)
Highbrow Crestfish
Lophotus cristatus Johnson

Distinguishing characters. — The silver-colored bandlike body of the crestfish is distinctive among the various bony fishes of the world. In life the dorsal, anal, and caudal fins are bright crimson, but the pectorals may be almost transparent. The forehead rises steeply, angling slightly anteriorly so as to resemble somewhat a dunce's cap.

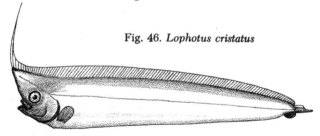

Fig. 46. *Lophotus cristatus*

Natural history notes. — Not many individuals of *Lophotus cristatus* have been seen off our shores and not all these were alive when found. One was caught near Santa Catalina Island in 1948 by an albacore fisherman who had spooled off about 300 feet of line and was fishing straight down. A year later, another was caught in the surf near Santa Monica. Several have been found since then, some in tuna stomachs, some washed ashore, and others swimming feebly at the surface. Over half of these came from the vicinity of Santa Catalina Island, but some came from nearly 800 miles offshore.

The largest individual was just under 40 inches in length and 6 pounds in weight. Nothing is known about crestfish ages, spawning habits, or migrations, but a larval specimen less than an inch long was cast ashore at La Jolla in December, 1905. This and a 2-inch long individual caught in a plankton net in December, 1962, indicate late summer or fall hatching. If the eggs require as long as ribbonfish eggs to hatch, spawning could take place in late spring or early summer.

The only food items noted in crestfish stomachs have been anchovies (bait and chum), hatchetfishes, and squid. A few parasitic roundworms were found in the stomach of one individual. Juvenile crestfish have twice been taken from the stomachs of bigeye tunas which were hooked on longline gear fishing several hundred feet beneath the surface.

A peculiarity of the crestfish is its ability to discharge, from a specialized internal gland, a dark ink-like fluid, similar to the "ink" ejected by an octopus or squid. Why a fish presumably living at a depth where little or no light penetrates would require, or need to use, a mechanism that manufactures and dispenses clouds of black "ink" remains a mystery. There is no indication that this fluid is luminescent.

Fishery information. — Only one of the crestfishes from off our coast was an authentic hook-and-line capture. Another that was said to have been hooked (by a surf fisherman), showed no hook marks in or around the mouth. Most likely it was cast ashore at the fisherman's feet or was seen swimming feebly in the surf, as were several adults reported from southern California. Offshore captures have been made in nets towed at fairly high speeds, and juveniles have been found in the stomachs of deep-feeding bigeye and albacore tunas.

Other family members. — A 4-foot individual swimming feebly in the surf at Long Beach in July, 1919, and subsequently captured, may have been a different species, since its forehead sloped backward rather than forward. Unfortunately the specimen cannot be found in any museum, and there is no record of what became of it. We do not know whether it was a different species or a variant of *L. cristatus*. Identical or closely related species are known from all temperate seas of the world.

Meaning of name. — *Lophotus* (crested) *cristatus* (also meaning crested).

TRACHIPTERIDAE (RIBBONFISH FAMILY)
Polka-dot Ribbonfish
Desmodema polystictum (Ogilby)

Distinguishing characters. — This is the only known ribbonfish that has an elongate ratlike tail. As a juvenile, its silvery body is freckled with dusky polka-dots, but these fade with age and none can be seen on the adult. The various fins (dorsal, pectorals, and pelvics) are generally crimson throughout life, but the dorsal fin grades into dusky, then almost black, on the tail. The pelvic fins become progressively shorter as the fish grows, and are lacking in the adult. Other changes occur as the fish becomes older: scales are present on the polka-dotted young but absent on the adult, and the steeply rising forehead slopes at a progressively lessened angle with age.

Natural history notes. — *Desmodema polystictum* is known from all tropic and temperate seas of the world, but apparently is not abundant anywhere. The largest complete specimen known, about 3½ feet long including the tail, weighed less than three-fourths

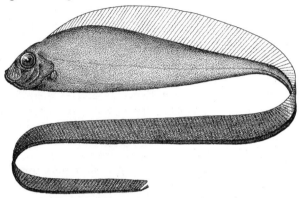

Fig. 47. *Desmodema polystictum*

of a pound. No data on growth rates or ages are available. Most individuals that were caught in their natural habitat seem to have been living 500 to 1,000 feet beneath the sea's surface. They feed upon an assortment of items found at these depths, including small fish, squids, octopuses, and crustaceans. Some spawning takes place during summer months, at least. Ribbonfish eggs have often been found in plankton nets; these eggs often require more than 50 days to hatch.

Fishery information. — Almost every year a few albacore fishermen, plying offshore waters, find polka-dotted juveniles lying on deck where they were spit up by fish they caught. Juveniles have been found in the stomachs of lancetfish and other predatory species caught in deep water on longline gear. Occasionally a purse-seine fisherman catches an adult in his net during nighttime fishing for tunas, but most adults are caught in midwater trawls towed 1,000 feet or more beneath the surface. A few adults, cast ashore on sandy or rocky beaches, have been found by early-morning strollers or fishermen.

Other family members. — Although there may be as many as ten kinds of ribbonfishes in the world, only four have been found off California. The commonest of these, *Trachipterus altivelis,* is known as the king-of-the-salmon. The name is derived from an Indian belief that these fish led salmon runs into the rivers each year. The silvery body of *T. altivelis* usually bears three to five large dark blotches anteriorly. The ventral profile is approximately straight (horizontal); the dorsal contour descends evenly and in a straight line from the crest of the head to the base of the tail, which rises at right angles to the body axis. Individuals are known to reach a length of 5½ feet, a weight of nine pounds, and the age of seven years. Many are caught or found each year in plankton nets, purse-seine gear, and albacore stomachs. One was even caught on a baited hook in Los Angeles Harbor. *Trachipterus fukuzakii* superficially resembles *T. altivelis* except for the straplike posterior third of its body: the dorsal and ventral contours converge behind the anal opening and then continue parallel to each other. It has been caught off California only once.

The other ribbonfish from our waters, *Zu cristatus,* has been found here only once (a 33-inch specimen, caught in 1932 off Newport Beach in a halibut net). The name "scalloped ribbonfish" fits juveniles very well: their bellies are scalloped for a short distance behind the pelvic fins, but the scalloping has all but disappeared in large adults. The sides of this species are crossed by numerous wavy dark bars, which are most distinct on young individuals.

Meaning of name. — *Desmodema* (band body) *polystictum* (many-spotted).

REGALECIDAE (OARFISH FAMILY)
Oarfish
Regalecus glesne (Ascanius)
Distinguishing characters. — The cockscomb-like anteriormost dorsal rays and the filamentous pelvic rays

with their terminal leaflike appendages are sufficient to distinguish this band-bodied oarfish from all other bony fishes. The silver body may be blotched or partially banded in dusky shades, and it may or may not terminate in a caudal fin. Although many oarfishes lose their posterior extremities at some time during their life, apparently they can survive with less than half their original or intended length. The dorsal fin is bright crimson.

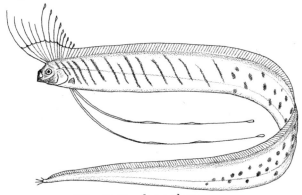

Fig. 48. *Regalecus glesne*

Natural history notes. — Fewer than five specimens of *Regalecus glesne* have ever been seen on our coast. The first of these, a 22-footer, drifted ashore at Newport Beach in 1901, where it created great interest among the populace for miles around. It was estimated to weigh several hundred pounds, and was the basis for many of the sea-serpent stories told by local bar patrons for more than a decade after its discovery. Some fifty years later, a fisherman standing on the rocky shore near Point Fermin (San Pedro) saw a 10-foot "monster" swimming feebly past several yards offshore. Fully clothed he jumped into the water and wrestled the beast ashore. It turned out to be the second-known oarfish from California, and, even with several feet of its tail missing, was an imposing sight.

The fisherman turned it over to the Cabrillo Beach Museum and a life-sized cast was made from it before the carcass was discarded. A few years later a 6-foot oarfish drifted ashore in Santa Monica Bay; and a 19-footer from near Topanga Canyon is preserved in the fish collections of the Los Angeles County Museum of Natural History. Smaller individuals have been found in the stomachs of deep-feeding tunas caught in tropical waters as far south as Chile.

The only food items found in the stomachs of these beasts have been shrimplike creatures known as euphausiids or krill. Over two quarts of these organisms, perhaps 10,000 individuals, were found in the stomach of the Point Fermin oarfish.

No information is available on ages, spawning season, migrations, or other habits. There are indications that the 22-foot Newport Beach specimen was just a "growing child." An incomplete oarfish reported from the Indian Ocean probably would have been about 35 feet long if it had not been partially eaten by a predator or predators at some earlier stage of its life.

Fishery information. — All the oarfishes found in our area had been cast ashore by the surf or were swimming feebly a few yards offshore. A few juveniles have been found in the stomachs of deep-feeding tunas and lancetfish, but not off California. A healthy oarfish in its native environment could probably evade a towed net, and from the food habits of these fish it is doubtful if one would take a hook. Larval specimens are sometimes captured in midwater trawls.

Other family members. — Similar or identical species are found in all temperate and tropic seas of the world, but are nowhere common. Perhaps as many have drifted ashore at Tasmania as at any place in the world.

Meaning of name. — *Regalecus* (king of the herring) *glesne* (origin uncertain, possibly the name of a person).

MELAMPHAIDAE (BIGSCALE FAMILY)
Crested Bigscale
Poromitra crassiceps (Günther)

Distinguishing characters. — The general body configuration, sculptured head, crestlike frontal ridges, and conspicuous internarial spine at the symphysis of paired nasals distinguish the crested bigscale from all other fishes in our area. It can be told from other California members of the genus by its 14 or more dorsal fin rays and moderately large eye, which goes about four times into the postorbital length of the head.

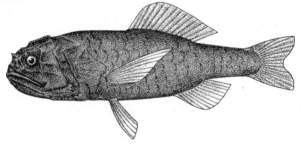

Fig. 49. *Poromitra crassiceps*

Natural history notes. — *Poromitra crassiceps* ranges from Alaska to mid-Chile (lat. 33° S.) and offshore for several hundred miles. Individuals have been captured in trawl nets that had been lowered more than 1,000 fathoms beneath the surface, but these specimens probably were netted at much shallower depths when the net was being lowered or raised. Most of the population is probably within 1,500 feet of the surface, migrating upward at night and downward just before daybreak. At maximum size the crested bigscale probably does not exceed 5½ or 6 inches in length and an ounce in weight. The otoliths are generally poor for determining age, but an examination of more than twenty sets representing an assortment of sizes leads us to believe that *P. crassiceps* reaches an age of at least ten years. Small crustaceans are the most abundant food items found in their stomachs.

A fossil melamphaid "imprint" (not *Poromitra*) was found in some Miocene diatomite beds near San Clemente, and fossil otoliths of melamphaids have been found in several Miocene, Pliocene, and Pleistocene deposits in southern California.

Fishery information. — Most captures have been made with midwater trawls being fished 800 feet or more beneath the surface. Bigscales rarely are taken in bottom trawls; such occurrences probably represent entrapment at shallower depths. We would anticipate their being found in the stomachs of larger predators, but know of only one such record — a salmon.

Other family members. — Three other genera of melamphaids involving six species are known to our waters. *Scopelogadus* can be distinguished among these because it has fewer than 15 rows of body scales; all others have more than 20. *Poromitra* has papery, crestlike frontal ridges, whereas *Melamphaes* and *Scopeloberyx* do not. *Scopeloberyx* has fewer than 15 elements in its dorsal fin; *Melamphaes* has 16 or more. Such characters as gill raker, fin ray, scale, and vertebral counts, the spination on head and opercle, and body proportions are useful in distinguishing the various species once a generic determination has been made.

Meaning of name. — *Poromitra* (pored headband, presumably in allusion to the crestlike frontal ridges and the numerous sensory pores on the sides of the head) *crassiceps* (thick head).

ANOPLOGASTERIDAE (FANGTOOTH FAMILY)
Fangtooth
Anoplogaster cornuta (Valenciennes)

Distinguishing characters. — The very large sculptured head, numerous long fangs in the jaws, dark granulose skin, and typical body shape distinguish

[94]

adult fangtooths from all other fishes in our waters. Juveniles have several elongate spines on their heads, are brownish in color, lack fangs in their jaws, and have a somewhat triangular body in cross section.

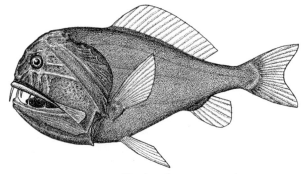

Fig. 50. *Anoplogaster cornuta*

Natural history notes. — *Anoplogaster cornuta* is found on both sides of the Atlantic and throughout much of the Pacific Ocean. Off our coast it ·ranges from British Columbia to south of the equator. At maximum size a fangtooth is about 6 inches long and weighs three to four ounces. The otoliths are so dense that it is difficult to distinguish growth zones, but those from a 5½-inch fangtooth had three quite good winter zones, indicating that it was at least three years old. The stomachs of several individuals have yielded an assortment of small crustaceans as well as small fishes and cephalopods. From an examination of internal anatomy, it appears that fangtooths spawn mostly during summer months in our area.

Although adult fangtooths were described in 1883, fifty years after Valenciennes named the "horned" juveniles, it was not until 1955 that both the juveniles and the adults were recognized as being *A. cornuta*. Between 1883 and 1955 the adults were known by the scientific name *Caulolepis longidens*.

Fishery information. — Midwater trawls are the only successful gear we know for capturing the fang-tooth. Most specimens netted off our coast appear to have been living at depths exceeding 2,000 feet. They are easy to keep alive in shipboard aquaria for as long as a week or ten days.

Other family members. — No other member of the family is known at present.

Meaning of name. — *Anoplogaster* (unarmed belly) *cornuta* (horned). This name aptly describes the juvenile but not the adult.

CHEILODIPTERIDAE (CARDINALFISH FAMILY)

Pelagic Basslet
Howella brodiei Ogilby

Distinguishing characters. — The pelagic basslet is the only small black fish in our waters with a bass-shaped body, a spiny opercle, and distinctive, widely separated dorsal fins. The rather elongate pectoral fin and firmly attached ctenoid scales on the body are additional helpful characters for recognizing it. Freshly caught individuals are silver-colored between the pelvic and anal fins.

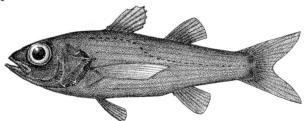

Fig. 51. *Howella brodiei*

Natural history notes. — The exact distribution of *Howella brodiei* is confused at present, but apparently includes much of the tropical Pacific Ocean (both north and south of the equator), the Indian Ocean and the north Atlantic, at least. On our coast it has been noted from north of San Francisco to central Baja California, although additional trawling should extend its range at least to mid-Chile. Usually it is caught 1,000 to 6,000 feet or more beneath the surface during daylight hours, but it approaches within 100 feet of the surface at night. The species probably attains a length of 4 inches or more, but nine out of ten individuals caught in our area are shorter than 3 inches. The otoliths of one that was just over 3 inches long had five winter rings; otoliths from smaller individuals had as many as three rings. We have no information on food habits or reproduction. The few stomachs we examined were empty.

Fishery information. — *H. brodiei* has been taken only with midwater trawls, and even in successful hauls it is unusual to find more than two or three individuals. The usual catch is comprised of a single specimen.

Other family members. — No other member of the family is known within several thousand miles of California.

Meaning of name. — *Howella* (for Lord Howe Island, the locality of capture for the first-named member of the genus) *brodiei* (probably named for a person).

BRAMIDAE (POMFRET FAMILY)
Bigscale Pomfret
Taractes longipinnis (Lowe)

Distinguishing characters. — The large prominent scales, the oval compressed body, the long falcate dorsal and anal fins (anteriorly), the deeply forked caudal fin, and the long pectorals distinguish the bigscale pomfret from all other fishes in our area.

Natural history notes. — Specimens of *Taractes longipinnis* apparently have been noted only four times in the eastern Pacific — all since April, 1953, all in the 80-mile stretch between Doheny State Park Beach and Redondo Beach, and all floundering or swimming feebly in the shallow surf. Elsewhere they are known from most world seas, both north and south of the equator. The largest of the four from California, a

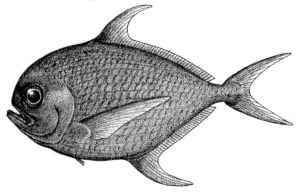

Fig. 52. *Taractes longipinnis*

2-footer, weighed 24 pounds, but it was not available for additional study. A 16½-inch fish, weighing 3 pounds, was about 18 months old, based upon an examination of its otoliths. A larger fish (20 inches long) appeared to have been eight years old, but could have been as much as two years younger or a year older. No information is at hand regarding food, spawning, or growth rates. Small individuals have been found in the stomachs of predatory fishes, but aside from parasites, disease, and man, adult bigscale pomfrets probably have few enemies.

Fishery information. — All the specimens captured in our waters were first observed floundering feebly in the surf, and were caught by hand. Two of the four were hauled ashore by small boys who were fishing or loafing nearby, and one by a woman who was strolling on the beach. Since other pomfrets are often caught on trolled lines or baited hooks, and with several types of nets, it is probable that the bigscale pomfret will also succumb to this gear.

Other family members. — Two other bramids occur

off our shores (*Brama japonica* and *Pteraclis velifera*), and at least two others (*Collybus drachme* and *Taractes asper*) have been captured not far from California waters. *Brama japonica* resembles *T. longipinnis* very closely, but has nearly twice as many scales along the lateral line (75 or more) as *Taractes* (about 40). *Pteraclis* has a more elongate body than *Brama* or *Taractes*, but its distinctive, long-rayed, fanlike dorsal and anal fins set it apart from other family members.

Meaning of name. — *Taractes* (a disturber, in reference to the difficulty of determining family relationships of the first specimen caught) *longipinnis* (long-finned).

CARISTIIDAE (MANEFISH FAMILY)
Veilfin
Caristius macropus (Bellotti)

Distinguishing characters. — The compressed body, high "forehead," elongate manelike dorsal fin, and long pelvic fins distinguish the veilfin from all other fishes in our waters. It is most likely to be confused

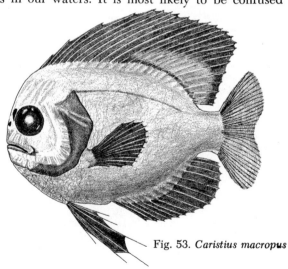

Fig. 53. *Caristius macropus*

with the bramid *Pteraclis velifera,* but the elongate pelvics preclude such a misidentification.

Natural history notes. — *Caristius macropus* ranges throughout the north Pacific Ocean and in other world seas as well, but it is rarely taken along our shores. One individual is known from off British Columbia and several from off California and northern Baja California, to about the latitude of Cedros Island. Veilfins are reported to reach a length of 12½ inches, but additional captures could include larger individuals. A 9-inch individual from off Eureka weighed exactly 8 ounces, and its otoliths indicated that it was five years old. No information is available regarding food habits except that fish remains have been noted in their stomachs. Juvenile veilfins, and probably adults too, are preyed upon by several larger fishes including albacore and lancetfish.

There is some question about where the manefish family fits into the scheme of things: some authors place it close to the bramids, others close to the stromateids, and so on. The otoliths (sagittae) suggest an affinity with zeomorph fishes.

The family is an ancient one, judged by several nearly intact veilfin "imprints" found in Miocene rocks in southern California.

Fishery information. — Almost all the known specimens of *C. macropus* on our coast have been taken with towed nets. Several were taken by personnel from scientific institutions using midwater trawls and plankton nets, but at least two were caught by commercial flatfish fishermen using otter trawls in depths of 1,000 feet or more.

Other family members. — One other veilfin believed to be *C. maderensis,* has been taken well offshore and to the south of California.

Meaning of name. — *Caristius* (top sail, in allusion to the sail-like dorsal fin) *macropus* (long foot, for the elongate pelvic fin).

PENTACEROTIDAE (PELAGIC ARMORHEAD FAMILY)

Pelagic Armorhead
Pentaceros richardsoni Smith

Distinguishing characters. — The unscaled, striated head bones, four anal fin spines, and laterally compressed body distinguish the pelagic armorhead from all other fishes in our area.

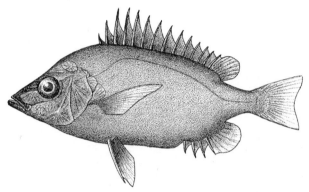

Fig. 54. *Pentaceros richardsoni*

Natural history notes. — In the north Pacific Ocean, specimens of *Pentaceros richardsoni* have been captured between about San Francisco and British Columbia, and across the ocean to Japan. Most occurrences have been considerable distances offshore. A 15-inch fish (from Japan) weighing just over two pounds appears to be a record size, although an unverified report gives 21 inches as a maximum. The three individuals from off California were all about the same length, 12 inches, and otoliths of two of these showed two excellent winter zones and opaque margins, indicating that each was about 30 months old. They did not appear to have spawned by that age. No information is available regarding spawning season, food habits, and other phases of life history.

Fishery information. — In the eastern north Pacific, most captures of *P. richardsoni* have been made with trawling gear being fished on the bottom. Since these fishes could have entered the net at any depth as it was being lowered or retrieved, it is not known whether they ever inhabit such depths. Many individuals have been captured in gill nets near the ocean's surface, and at least one pelagic armorhead was dipnetted at the surface by personnel aboard one of our weather ships.

Other family members. — No other close relative of *P. richardsoni* is found within several thousand miles of California.

Meaning of name. — *Pentaceros* (five-horned) *richardsoni* (for John Richardson, naturalist and explorer).

URANOSCOPIDAE (STARGAZER FAMILY)
Smooth Stargazer
Kathetostoma averruncus Jordan and Bollman

Distinguishing characters. — The scaleless body, and large, broad head with the eyes placed anteriorly and somewhat dorsal, in conjunction with a nearly vertical mouth, distinguish the smooth stargazer from all other California fishes. Additional distinctive characters include broad pectoral fins, a heavy backward-pointing spine on each side above the gill opening, and a dorsal fin without spines.

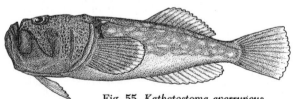

Fig. 55. *Kathetostoma averruncus*

Natural history notes. — Specimens of *Kathetostoma averruncus* have been recorded in the eastern Pacific between Piedras Blancas, California, and Panama, but they are not common north of Magdalena Bay, Baja California. About a dozen individuals are known from California, where they were caught on the bottom in depths of 60 to 800 feet or more. Larvae and young of *K. averruncus* apparently live at or near the surface, and in this environment they are capable of swimming or drifting many hundreds of miles with prevailing oceanic currents.

The largest of those from California (or elsewhere) was 12¼ inches long and weighed 1 pound 15 ounces. This female, when it was caught in March, released quantities of mature eggs. The otoliths had nine winter zones, and there were signs that it had first spawned in its third year. The bulk of the food items found in smooth stargazer stomachs has been other fish, usually bottom dwellers, including sculpins (Cottidae), a small lingcod, a combfish, a sanddab, a rockfish, and an anchovy. One stargazer had eaten a small octopus as well as a couple of small fishes.

Fishery information. — All but one of the smooth stargazers from off our coast were caught in trawl nets which were being dragged along the bottom. This gear (shrimp nets) has made most of the stargazer captures in more southerly waters also. The largest fish from California was caught on a baited hook being fished on or near the bottom. Larvae and young are frequently dipnetted at the surface (at night they are attracted to bright lights suspended above the water from drifting vessels), and tuna fishermen regularly find them on deck where they have been regurgitated by fish they have caught.

Other family members. — A close relative of *K. averruncus* has been captured in central Baja California waters, but this fish (genus *Astroscopus*) is scaled and has a spinous dorsal fin.

Meaning of name. — *Kathetostoma* (vertical mouth) *averruncus* (a deity which wards off; so named because of the heavily boned skull).

CHIASMODONTIDAE (SWALLOWER FAMILY)
Needletooth Swallower
Kali normani (Parr)

Distinguishing characters. — The jaws and stomachs of swallowers are constructed in such a way that extremely large prey can be engulfed, sometimes even those exceeding the size of the predator. The elongated body, fin placement and sizes, double row of formidable fanglike teeth, arched jaws that fail to close entirely, lack of photophores, and smooth skin (without spines) in the tail region distinguish the needletooth swallowers from other species of swallowers.

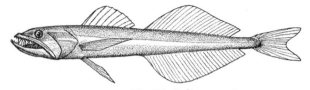

Fig. 56. *Kali normani*

Natural history notes. — *Kali normani* ranges from the vicinity of San Pedro, California, to that of Cape San Lucas, Baja California (at least). Judged by its rarity in midwater trawl catches, it apparently is one of the minor constituents comprising the deep scattering layers. Individuals have been captured at night as shallow as 1,500 feet beneath the surface, but, since the nets used in their capture were fishing continuously while they were in the water, these specimens could have been netted much closer to the surface.

All the needletooth swallowers we have seen were shorter than 6 inches and weighed less than an ounce. On the otoliths of several large individuals up to four winter zones could be discerned. If all annuli were noted, and none was masked or hidden at the otolith margin, these fish apparently do not reach a very old age, or else the largest (oldest) adults are not being captured. Their stomachs have yielded mostly fish remains, but some crustaceans also have been observed. No information is available on spawning season or habits, and other phases of their life history.

Fishery information. — We do not know any reason, why the swallowers would not make a good meal for a larger bathypelagic predator, but we have never heard of one being found in the stomach of such a fish. To our knowledge, all captures have been made with midwater trawls and similar gear being fished by personnel from one of our scientific institutions.

Other family members. — Three other swallowers belonging to two genera have been captured off our coast. *Chiasmodon niger* superficially resembles *Kali*, but it has well-developed pseudobranchia, jaws that meet when closed, shorter pectorals (barely equal body depth), and its anteriormost jaw teeth are longest. *Pseudoscopelus* has photophores (*Kali and Chiasmodon* do not) and on *P. scriptus* these reach the ventral fin and a few are found along the lowermost ray of this fin. In *P. altipinnis* the photophores extend only to the ventral fin insertion. The otoliths of *Pseudoscopelus* are so different from those of *Kali* and *Chiasmodon* that we question its familial placement — perhaps it should stand alone as some ichthyologists have suggested after studying other anatomical features.

Meaning of name. — *Kali* (the Hindu goddess of creation and destruction) *normani* (for John R. Norman, 1899-1944, a noted British ichthyologist).

ICOSTEIDAE (RAGFISH FAMILY)
Ragfish
Icosteus aenigmaticus Lockington

Distinguishing characters. — The general shape of the spotted young ragfish cannot be mistaken for any other marine species in our area, especially when its soft flabbiness is taken into consideration. The adult is brownish (without spots), thick-skinned, oblong-elliptical, and has a slightly forked tail, but the very flabby body and troutlike head are still quite apparent. Pelvic fins are missing in the adult.

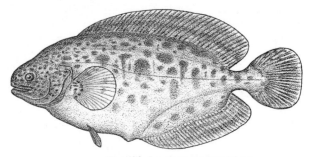

Fig. 57. *Icosteus aenigmaticus*

Natural history notes. — *Icosteus aenigmaticus* ranges from northern Alaska to San Onofre, California, and across the north Pacific to Japan. Juveniles are spotted (as figured) and supposedly inhabit great depths, but fair numbers have been captured in relatively shallow water near the shore or near the surface offshore. Adults apparently do live in deep water, if reliance can be placed upon capture methods and gear. The largest measured individual was 6 feet 10 inches long, but larger specimens have been taken. A 5-foot 3-inch female caught off Eureka in July, 1966, weighed 54 pounds. The ovaries were filled with nearly ripe eggs, indicating summer spawning.

An examination of otoliths of several ragfish 10 inches to 5 feet long indicates that the spotted phase lasts less than a year. When these fishes grow to be 10 to 12 inches long, they probably move offshore to areas that are seldom fished, for not many are captured until they are 2 feet long or longer. A few individuals 2 to 2½ feet long have been caught near the surface in salmon gill nets about halfway across the north Pacific. Growth is quite rapid during the first two years, and spawning probably occurs in the third or fourth summer. Most of the 4- to 5-foot adults captured off California are females nearly ready to spawn. These 7- to 9-year-old fish apparently enter our coastal fishing grounds for spawning purposes.

The only individuals examined for food had eaten small fishes, squids, and octopuses. Large ragfish have been found in the stomachs of several sperm whales.

Fishery information. — Spotted juveniles show up frequently in trawl catches, but gill nets and purse seines also have yielded fair numbers. There is at least one record of a juvenile ragfish being caught on hook and line. The Japanese occasionally catch adult ragfish in gill nets, but all the large fish we have seen were caught in trawl nets being fished on the bottom in depths of 45 to 200 or more fathoms (270 to 1,200 feet). One or two large ragfish have been cast ashore by stormy seas.

Other family members. — *I. aenigmaticus* is the only member of this family known.

Meaning of name. — *Icosteus* (literally, a fish with yielding bones, alluding to its flabby raglike consistency) *aenigmaticus* (puzzling) — a puzzling fish with a flabby body.

TRICHIURIDAE (CUTLASSFISH FAMILY)
Black Scabbardfish
Lepidopus xantusi Goode and Bean

Distinguishing characters. — The body shape of the black scabbardfish and the fact that it is about

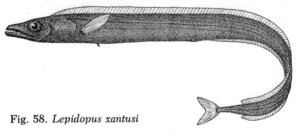

Fig. 58. *Lepidopus xantusi*

15 times as long as deep, and has a deeply forked mackerel-like tail distinguish it from all others off our coast.

Natural history notes. — *Lepidopus xantusi* ranges from Eureka to Mazatlán, Mexico, at least. Silver-colored juveniles up to 12 inches long apparently live near the surface, but adults have always been captured quite deep. Those caught on hook and line have been 350 to 1,650 feet beneath the surface, usually at or near the bottom. The largest measured individual was 35½ inches long, although one "about 40 inches long" was noted in the San Pedro fresh fish markets many years ago. At maximum length a black scabbardfish weighs barely three pounds. The otoliths show growth zones very well, and several 2½ footers were 15 to 17 years old.

Spawning probably takes place in late spring and early summer, judged by the gonads of numerous individuals. Stomachs have yielded a wide variety of food items, mostly inch-long euphausiids (shrimplike organisms), small Pacific hake, and anchovies.

Fishery information. — Large scabbardfish have been found floating at the ocean's surface, washed ashore, and in the stomachs of deep-feeding tunas, but most have been caught in otter trawls fished at or near the bottom. One trawlerman caught one and a half tons of them in a single haul of his net in 840 feet of water during April, 1962. Sport and commercial fishermen catch *L. xantusi* occasionally, especially if they have 800 feet or more of line out. One fisherman caught five large adults in two hours while fishing near the bottom in very deep water. Silver-colored juveniles have been found in the stomachs of adults, and caught in an assortment of nets: surface trawls, purse seines, bait nets, and others. A scabbardfish "imprint" (probably not *L. xantusi*) has been found in a Miocene diatomite quarry near Lompoc.

Other family members. — Two other members of

this family are found in our waters. *Trichiurus nitens,* the Pacific cutlassfish, is similar to *Lepidopus* in body shape, but lacks a distinct caudal fin, its body tapering to a hairlike extremity. The razorback scabbardfish, *Assurger anzac,* has a tail like *Lepidopus,* but can be recognized by the extreme length of its body, which is 25 times as long as deep.

Meaning of name. — *Lepidopus* (scale foot, in allusion to the scalelike pelvic fins) *xantusi* (for John Xantus de Vasey, who collected the first specimen).

GEMPYLIDAE (SNAKE MACKEREL FAMILY)
Snake Mackerel
Gempylus serpens Cuvier

Distinguishing characters. — The two lateral lines and five to seven dorsal and anal finlets distinguish the snake mackerel from all other elongate straplike fishes with mackerel-like tails, and no other fish anywhere has this combination of characters.

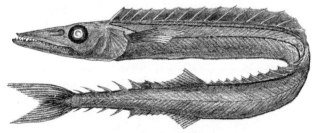

Fig. 59. *Gempylus serpens*

Natural history notes. — *Gempylus serpens,* known in all tropic seas of the world, occasionally strays into temperate waters. In the eastern Pacific it has been taken or observed at numerous localities between San Pedro, California, and central Chile. Usually it is seen at the ocean's surface, but tuna longliners sometimes catch large individuals several hundred feet beneath the surface, and their remains have been found in the stomachs of deep-feeding predators. The single specimen from California was 23 inches long and weighed about five ounces. Its otoliths appeared to have two winter rings, and the otoliths of a 5-footer seemed to have five rings, but we do not feel confident of these ages. We have found only fish remains in the few snake mackerel stomachs that contained food.

Fishery information. — The only individual known from our waters was picked up in a rocky pool (still alive) where it apparently had been cast by breaking waves. Its occurrence in shallow, near-shore waters indicates that it was probably not a healthy fish. From the vicinity of Turtle Bay, Baja California, south, tuna fishermen often see snake mackerel swimming around their ships at night, and occasional specimens are washed aboard and are found on deck in the morning. The snake mackerel is publicized as one of the supposedly extremely rare species that washed aboard the *Kon Tiki* during its spectacular voyage across the Pacific. Large individuals are sometimes caught on longline gear fished well beneath the surface. Snake mackerel of all sizes are occasionally found in the stomachs of such predatory species as tunas and marlins.

Other family members. — Two other members of the family have been recorded from California; the oilfish, *Ruvettus pretiosus,* from Encinitas in 1932 and off Marineland of the Pacific in 1967, and the escolar, *Lepidocybium flavobrunneum,* from Long Beach in 1932 and from near Redondo Beach in 1960. The oilfish is blackish, rather flabby, somewhat mackerel-shaped, with sharp, osseus spicules or tubercles projecting from its scales. Its lateral line is obsolete. The brownish escolar has an even more mackerel-shaped body, a well-developed keel on each side of the caudal peduncle, and a lateral line that undulates along the fish's entire side.

Meaning of name. — *Gempylus* (an ancient name of a scombroid fish) *serpens* (a snake).

LUVARIDAE (LOUVAR FAMILY)
Louvar
Luvarus imperialis Rafinesque

Distinguishing characters. — The tunalike outline, dolphinfish-like head, crimson fins, and frothy pink body (silver when dead) distinguish the juvenile and adult louvar from all other fishes. Its bones are cartilaginous or weakly ossified, and break, tear, or pull apart when any strain is placed upon them.

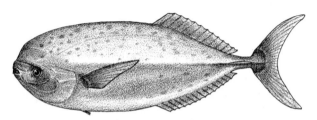

Fig. 60. *Luvarus imperialis*

Natural history notes. — On our coast, specimens of *Luvarus imperialis* have been reported from Acapulco, Mexico, and Newport, Oregon, but most of the fifty or more known individuals have been from the area between San Diego and Monterey. Louvars inhabit most other world seas, but do not seem to be as abundant elsewhere as off California. Our purse-seine fisheries probably account for the record of their abundance in our waters.

If such records were kept in the world, California apparently would hold them for both the longest louvar (a 6-foot 2-inch fish from off Huntington Beach in 1955) and the heaviest (a 305-pounder, washed ashore at Redondo Beach in 1932). Louvar otoliths are very tiny and do not provide any indication of age.

The louvar feeds primarily upon jellyfishes and similar gelatinous planktonic forms. In order to derive maximum food value from these, the digestive tract is modified in several ways: the stomach is lined with many elongate, nipple-like projections, which increase the absorptive surface, and the intestine is very long and convoluted. A 40-inch fish, which weighed 45 pounds, had a 37-foot intestine. Only a few individuals examined have had any food in their stomachs, and this has consisted of jellyfish, ctenophores (comb jellies), pyrosomes, and one small fish.

The ovaries of a 295-pound female that washed ashore at Morro Bay in May, 1953, were enlarged and contained nearly ripe eggs. This would indicate late spring or early summer spawning in our area. Nothing is known about growth rates or ages, but an 8-inch louvar found in the stomach of a wahoo at Clarion Island, Mexico, in April, 1953, could have been from the previous year's hatch.

Fishery information. — Most of our local louvars have been caught at night by purse-seine vessels fishing for bluefin tuna, especially near San Clemente Island. Many have been cast ashore where they were **found** by beach strollers or fishermen; others have been picked up at sea where they were drifting dead at the surface or floundering in a feeble condition. A couple have been reported as having been hooked, but such reports are extremely doubtful because of the weakly constructed jaws and other bones. One louvar was caught in a shark net, one was killed by an underwater explosion, and one was found in a wahoo stomach. The louvar has very delicate white flesh and is considered tasty by those privileged to try some.

Other family members. — *L. imperialis* is the only known member of the family, but because of the metamorphosis its odd-shaped larva goes through, and its world distribution, many other scientific names have been given to it.

Meaning of name. — *Luvarus* (silver?) *imperialis* (emperor).

TETRAGONURIDAE (SQUARETAIL FAMILY)
Smalleye Squaretail
Tetragonurus cuvieri Risso

Distinguishing characters. — The dark cigar-shaped body covered with tightly adhering ridged scales, and the two pairs of caudal keels distinguish the smalleye squaretail from all other fishes.

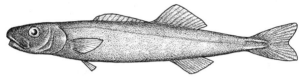

Fig. 61. *Tetragonurus cuvieri*

Natural history notes. — On our coast *Tetragonurus cuvieri* has been reported from south of the Aleutians and from off British Columbia to the latitude of Cedros Island, Baja California. It is known also from the central and western north Pacific, the eastern north Atlantic, and off Australia and New Zealand. Most captures appear to have been made well offshore within 150 feet of the surface.

The largest specimen of *T. cuvieri* from the eastern north Pacific was a 15-incher removed from the mouth of a Pacific halibut caught off Eureka in 1949. A New Zealand specimen at 24½ inches seems to be the largest ever noted, although some of the 146 specimens caught south of the Aleutians during 1955 may have been larger. Unfortunately, the only indication of size for these squaretails is a note by the author who reported their capture that most of them exceeded 250 millimeters (10 inches) in total length.

The life history of the squaretail is not well known. Ages have not been satisfactorily determined, but from an examination of otoliths from a few individuals it appears that 10- to 12-inch fish are three to four years old, and 14-inch fish are five to six years old. A 14-inch female that was caught off Point Arguello in September, 1958, weighed barely half a pound; this fish appeared to be about ready to spawn. In the Mediterranean, *T. cuvieri* is believed to spawn throughout the year.

The only food items reported from squaretail stomachs have been jellyfishes and ctenophores (comb jellies). Both the jaw structure and digestive system of *Tetragonurus* seem particularly well adapted to such a diet. In the Mediterranean the flesh of *T. cuvieri* is considered toxic, supposedly because it feeds upon jellyfishes, many of which have venomous stinging cells. Tests conducted on the flesh of California specimens failed to show that these were toxic.

Fishery information. — Perhaps 40 to 50 juvenile to adult smalleye squaretails have been noted in the eastern north Pacific since the first one was taken in 1919 (not including the 146 caught in surface gill nets south of the Aleutians in 1955). Perhaps two-thirds of the 40 to 50 specimens were recovered by albacore fishermen, after having been regurgitated by fish they had caught. Most of the rest have been captured by fishery workers and other scientific personnel during offshore investigations, but at least one squaretail was picked up on a beach floundering in the wash of a receding wave, and other specimens have been found in stomachs of Pacific halibut and lancetfish. One fish was snagged on a trolled albacore jig, and a squaretail was found in the stomach of a fur seal.

Other family members. — Two other species of *Tetragonurus* are known from various oceans of the world, but neither has been reported within several thousand miles of California.

Meaning of name. — *Tetragonurus* (square-tailed) *cuvieri* (in honor of Georges Chrétien Leopold Dagobert Cuvier, 1769-1832, the great comparative anatomist who laid the foundations of modern ichthyology).

CENTROLOPHIDAE (MEDUSAFISH FAMILY)
Medusafish
Icichthys lockingtoni (Jordan and Gilbert)

Distinguishing characters. — Although the body shape of the medusafish changes with age, the changes are not sufficient to prevent identification at any size. Juveniles lack scales, are a transparent pinkish color, and have a rather evenly rounded snout; older individuals are completely covered with tiny scales, have dusky bodies, and a troutlike snout (more squared-off than in juveniles). Medusaefish of all sizes are soft-bodied, limp and flexible; the spinous and soft-rayed parts of the dorsal fin are almost indistinguishable except by critical examination.

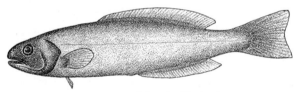

Fig. 62. *Icichthys lockingtoni*

Natural history notes. — *Icichthys lockingtoni* ranges from the Gulf of Alaska to central Baja California and offshore throughout the north Pacific to Japan. The largest individual from our coast seems to be a 16-inch fish caught with a midwater trawl off northern California in September, 1967. This fish, a female weighing one-and-a-quarter pounds, was nearly ready to spawn; its stomach contained euphausiid and jellyfish remains. There is a record of an 18-inch specimen from Japan. Efforts to determine the ages of medusaefish have not been successful.

Juveniles (up to 3 or 4 inches, at least) usually associate with jellyfishes, apparently taking advantage of the protection afforded by the jellyfish against predators. It is thought by many that medusaefish are immune to the jellyfish's venomous stinging cells, whereas species that might prey upon them are not, but this has not always proved true. Most references to their "commensal" behavior suggest that medusae-fish feed upon "crumbs" dropped by the jellyfishes, but there is little factual information on their food habits. There is some evidence that they occasionally nip pieces from their protective host. Large medusae-fish may move out on their own for solitary individuals are usually caught when no jellyfishes are nearby. A single otolith of *I. lockingtoni* has been identified from a San Pedro fossil deposit of early Pleistocene age.

Fishery information. — Juveniles are abundant off our coast during much of the year. They are easily captured with plankton nets and in midwater trawls, particularly when this gear is operated near the surface. Many have been dipnetted, captured in purse seines and bait nets, or regurgitated by predatory species. A few have been picked up on the beach where they were cast by the waves, and at least one was caught in a beach seine.

Other family members. — No other member of the family is known to our coast.

Meaning of name. — *Icichthys* (alluding to a fish with a flexible skeleton) *lockingtoni* (for W. N. Lockington, its discoverer, who was then ichthyologist for the California Academy of Sciences).

NOMEIDAE (FLOTSAMFISH FAMILY)
Blackrag
Psenes pellucidus Lütken

Distinguishing characters. — Because of its soft, flexible, characteristically-shaped body, the blackrag might be mistaken for two other species that inhabit our waters (*Icosteus aenigmaticus* and *Icichthys lockingtoni*), but no others. Its separate dorsal fins distinguish it from both of these, however.

Natural history notes. — *Psenes pellucidus* ranges

throughout tropical, semitropical, and temperate oceanic realms of the Atlantic, Pacific, and Indian oceans. On our coast it has been captured only once,

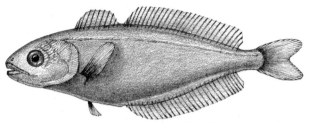

Fig. 63. *Psenes pellucidus*

an 18-incher caught off Newport Beach. We have found no reports of any larger blackrags. The young of these fishes seem to be most abundant in offshore tropical waters, where they live at or near the surface, usually in association with floating debris, kelp, and similar objects. Larger individuals apparently live deeper in the water column, and thus are not found near floating material. The stomachs of these fishes have contained an assortment of food items, particularly small crustaceans and fishes, including eggs and larvae. *Psenes* is fed upon by many predators, including birds during their early life near the surface of the sea. No information is available on age, or spawning season and habits.

Fishery information. — Juveniles are easily dipnetted from under and around floating objects in tropical waters and two were recently taken off northern Baja California in a midwater trawl being towed near the surface. Adults are seldom seen or captured. Intermediate sizes are often found in the stomachs of oceanic predators such as lancetfishes, tunas, and jacks. The Newport Beach fish was captured in a bait net in relatively shallow water, not far from the head of a submarine canyon.

Other family members. — Only one other nomeid,

Cubiceps gracilis, has been captured off California. This fish, a 27-incher weighing six pounds, was easily distinguished by its elongate cigar-shaped body and very long pectoral fins.

Meaning of name. — *Psenes* (pertaining to the osprey *Pandion;* the logic behind this name is not clear) *pellucidus* (transparent).

ZANIOLEPIDIDAE (COMBFISH FAMILY)
Shortspine Combfish
Zaniolepis frenata Eigenmann

Distinguishing characters. — The shagreen-like texture of the skin of the shortspine combfish, resulting from the minute, imbricated, very rough scales, is in itself sufficient for identification. The small mouth, the almost round, tapering body, and the placement, extent, shape, and color (black spots and streaks interspersed with lemon-yellow areas) of the dorsal and anal fins clinch the identification.

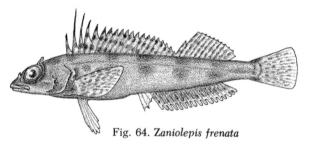

Fig. 64. *Zaniolepis frenata*

Natural history notes. — *Zaniolepis frenata* ranges from somewhere off southern Oregon to Cedros Island, Baja California. Tiny juveniles have been caught many miles offshore where depths may exceed 1,000 fathoms, but adults are almost always caught on the bottom in 180 to 800 feet or more. A large individual might be 10 inches long and weigh 4 or 5 ounces. An examination of otoliths indicates that combfish attain the age of ten or eleven years; the largest and oldest individuals are almost invariably females. Polychaete worms seem to be the preferred food, but euphausiids, amphipods, and fish eggs have been found in their stomachs. Spawning appears to take place in late fall and winter.

A single otolith of a related species, Z. *latipinnis,* has been reported from the Pleistocene of southern California.

Fishery information. — The adults have been caught on hook and line in moderately deep water, but only when tiny hooks were being used. They are abundant in trawl catches from 50 to 100 fathoms or more, where the bottom is muddy. This mud usually sticks to their sandpapery skin, and when the catch is dumped from the trawl net, the mud-covered combfishes assume a characteristic horseshoe-shaped pose and lie on the deck as if in a trance. Combfishes are frequently found in the stomachs of rockfishes and other bottom-feeding predators.

Other family members. — Z. *latipinnis* is the only other combfish in our waters. The second dorsal spine of this species is very long (almost filamentous). It lacks a cirrus over the eye, and its body and fin colors include shades of red not found in the shortspine combfish. It also inhabits shallower depths.

Meaning of name. — *Zaniolepis* (comb scale, for the shagreen-like texture of the skin) *frenata* (bridled, in reference to the body and fin coloring).

AGONIDAE (POACHER FAMILY)
Blacktip Poacher
Xeneretmus latifrons (Gilbert)

Distinguishing characters. — A combination of characters that distinguish the blacktip poacher from all other fishes includes an elongate, tapering body covered with spiny, platelike scales in longitudinal rows, the lack of a deep pit in the top of the head behind the eyes, the presence of a small plate on the tip of the snout with a single erect spine in its center (another spine points backward at each corner of this plate), and blackish pigment on the distal third of each dorsal fin.

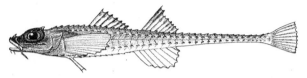

Fig. 65. *Xeneretmus latifrons*

Natural history notes. — Specimens of *Xeneretmus latifrons* are abundant in much of the area between Cape Colnett, Baja California, and northern British Columbia. They live on the bottom in 60 to more than 1,200 feet of water (10 to 218 fathoms), generally occurring in shallower water to the north. Spawning apparently takes place during spring months, and the newly hatched larvae of some poachers lead a pelagic existence, living nearer the surface than the bottom. The otoliths of a near-record female 7 inches long and weighing one ounce, had six winter zones, indicating that the species lives at least six years. The food of *X. latifrons* consists almost exclusively of tiny shrimplike creatures (crustaceans) mainly mysids. Blacktip poachers in turn have been eaten by a few bottom-dwelling predators, mostly flatfishes and hake; one lancetfish had made part of a meal on *Xeneretmus*.

Otoliths of poachers, probably *X. latifrons* for the most part, have been found in several Pliocene and Pleistocene deposits in southern California.

Fishery information. — Postlarval poachers are sometimes captured in plankton nets near the surface, but adults are captured only with such bottom-fishing gear as shrimp trawls and otter trawls. Poacher remains are occasionally found in the stomachs of predatory fishes.

Other family members. — Thirteen other agonids have been reported from our waters. Although their resemblance to *X. latifrons* makes it easy to assign them to the family Agonidae, a wide assortment of external characters has been used to distinguish the different genera and species.

Meaning of name. — *Xeneretmus* (strange or peculiar oar, apparently in allusion to the outline of the body) *latifrons* (wide forehead).

LIPARIDIDAE (SNAILFISH FAMILY)
Blacktail Snailfish
Careproctus melanurus Gilbert

Distinguishing characters. — The small suction disk on the underside beneath the eyes, the pink body, black posterior dorsal and anal fins, and black caudal fin are sufficient to distinguish this loose-skinned, semigelatinous blacktail snailfish from all its relatives in our waters, as well as from nonrelated species.

Fig. 66. *Careproctus melanurus*

Natural history notes. — *Careproctus melanurus* ranges from northern British Columbia to Santa Catalina Island, at least. It lives at or near the bottom, being most abundant on a muddy substrate in depths of 300 to 5,000 feet, at least. A near-record 10¼-incher weighed slightly more than half a pound. An examination of numerous otoliths revealed that some individuals reach an age of at least six or seven years. A few scattered notes indicate that snailfish feed upon polychaete worms, small crustaceans, tiny clams, and similar items, but no details are available on most other phases of their life history.

[121]

Fishery information. — Blacktail snailfish are fairly common constituents of trawl catches made at depths exceeding 600 feet, and occasionally they turn up in stomachs of such bottom-feeding predators as hake, arrowtooth flounders, and rockfish.

Other family members. — Possibly eighteen to twenty other liparids belonging to six or more genera have been reported from waters off our coast. Many of these are known from only one specimen and from depths exceeding 6,000 feet; so there is little reliable information on how to distinguish them. Several genera do not have a ventral disk (*Lipariscus, Nectoliparis, Paraliparis,* and *Rhinoliparis*), whereas *Careproctus* and *Liparis* do have adhesive ventral disks. In *Liparis* the disk is behind the gill slits; in *Careproctus* it is in front of these. The size of the adhesive disk, length and position of the gill openings, position of the anus, posterior termination of the dorsal and anal fins, presence or absence of head spines, and fin-ray counts are important in distinguishing the various species.

Meaning of name. — *Careproctus* (head anus, alluding to the anal opening being well forward in the head region) *melanurus* (black tail).

LOPHIIDAE (GOOSEFISH FAMILY)
Threadfin Goosefish
Chirolophius spilurus (Garman)

Distinguishing characters. — The troughlike, concave face, the very broad mouth with bands of relatively long, depressible teeth, the fleshy papillae or filaments scattered over the body, the double series of elongate, filamentous dorsal spines which lack terminal fleshy baits, and the simple humeral spine distinguish the threadfin goosefish from all other species inhabiting our waters.

Natural history notes. — *Chirolophius spilurus* ranges from Panama (at least) northward throughout the Gulf of California, and on the outer coast to the vicinity of Santa Barbara. As adults they inhabit muddy bottom areas, usually in depths exceeding 600 feet.

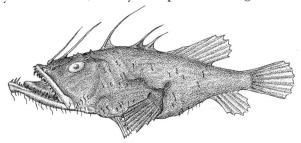

Fig. 67. *Chirolophius spilurus*

An 11-inch individual (about maximum size) trawled near Conception Bay in the Gulf of California was seven years old, judged by growth zones visible on its otoliths, and weighed about a pound.

Juveniles undergo a pelagic existence, being found at or near the surface, often many miles offshore and over extremely great depths. They are attracted to bright lights suspended above the surface at night, and can then be easily dipnetted. Tunas and similar predators living in these offshore pelagic waters frequently feed upon juvenile anglerfishes.

The adults feed mostly upon small bottom-dwelling fishes, but crustaceans have been found in their stomachs, and it is very likely that they eat other kinds of food also. We have no information on spawning habits, behavior, or other phases of their life history.

Fishery information. — Tuna fishermen often observe or collect the pelagic juveniles, but adults are seldom captured except with bottom trawling gear. In tropical waters, shrimp fishermen often catch one or two individuals per haul when operating in depths exceeding 100 fathoms. There seems to be only one record (unpublished) of *C. spilurus* in our waters.

Other family members. — This is the only member

of the family known in our waters. A near-relative, *Lophiomus caulinaris*, inhabits much the same range as *C. spilurus,* but can be distinguished readily by its three-pronged humeral spine and the modified fleshy tip on the filamentous first dorsal spine. *L. caulinaris* does not have a pelagic juvenile stage, and adults usually inhabit shallower depths than *C. spilurus.*

Meaning of name. — *Chirolophius* (a *Lophius* with pectoral fins) *spilurus* (spotted tail).

OGCOCEPHALIDAE (BATFISH FAMILY)
Spotted Batfish
Zalieutes elater (Jordan and Gilbert)

Distinguishing characters. — The bizarre shape of this dorsoventrally flattened fish distinguishes it from all other California marine teleosts. The overhanging snout, the short bulbous illicium above the mouth, and the yellowish black-rimmed "bulls-eyes" on the back are additional useful characters in identifying the spotted batfish.

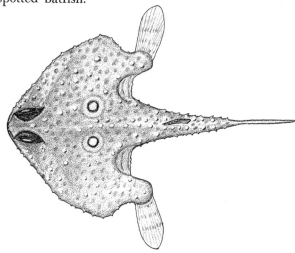

Fig. 68. *Zalieutes elater*

Natural history notes. — *Zalieutes elater* ranges from Point Conception to Panama, but is not common on the outer coast north of Cape San Lucas, Baja California. Batfishes live on the bottom, where they use their strongly developed pectoral fins for "walking" around. The few individuals caught off our shores apparently were no deeper than about 150 feet. A large individual might be 6 inches long and weigh a couple of ounces, but we have no accurate information on maximum size or weight. Otoliths from fairly large adults indicate that they attain an age of at least nine years. The few stomachs we have examined contained tiny crustaceans and fish remains, but they probably eat most other available food items of the right size. Nothing is known regarding their reproductive habits.

Fishery information. — In Mexican and Central American waters, spotted batfish are common in catches made with shrimp trawls and bait nets that drag the bottom. A skindiver occasionally observes one creeping along the bottom, and beach strollers sometimes find the mummified remains of batfish which have been cast ashore by stormy seas. Off our coast, batfish have been caught in halibut nets and purse seines.

Other family members. — No other member of this family is known within several thousand miles of California.

Meaning of name. — *Zalieutes* (*zale*, surge of the sea; *halieutes*, fisher) *elater* (for a beetle that has eye-like spots on its back).

CAULOPHRYNIDAE (FANFIN FAMILY)
Fanfin
Caulophryne jordani Goode and Bean

Distinguishing characters. — The enormously elongated rays of the dorsal, anal, and pectoral fins distinguish these anglerfishes from other forms. The absence of a distal bait (esca) on the tip of the fishing pole (illicium) is unique among anglerfishes. The bodies of adults are covered with small filaments. As in most ceratioid anglerfishes, the musculature is feeble, and the skeleton is poorly ossified.

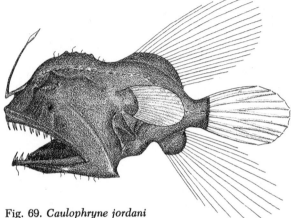

Fig. 69. *Caulophryne jordani*

Natural history notes. — Fewer than thirty specimens of *Caulophryne jordani* are known from throughout the world, including from the north Atlantic, off southern California, the Gulf of Panama, the south Pacific, the Indo-Malaya sea, the Tasman Sea, and the Indian Ocean. The largest known individual was slightly more than 8 inches long.

Although the lightly pigmented larvae of *C. jordani* have not been recorded off California, they are readily distinguished from all other anglerfish larvae by the high number of dorsal and anal rays and by the presence of ventral fins. Especially conspicuous are the colossal pectoral fins.

Males and females are similar when young, but upon metamorphosis the fishing pole develops only in female individuals, a rather striking example of sexual dimorphism.

Typical of three other families of anglerfishes, the males of *C. jordani* are parasitic on the females. The much smaller male (a mature individual is less than an inch long) seeks out a female, attaches to her, and undergoes rather drastic changes. Prior to attachment, *C. jordani* males appear much the same as females, except for being somewhat thinner. Males also have slightly smaller eyes, strongly developed olfactory organs, and are usually toothless.

Fishery information. — All known individuals have been captured in midwater trawls and plankton nets during exploratory fishing operations by scientific personnel. Successful hauls have yielded fanfins from as shallow as 35 feet and as deep as 4,000 feet.

Other family members. — There is no other family member, but three subspecies are recognized in a recent revision of the family.

Meaning of name. — *Caulophryne* (stem frog, in allusion to its primitive position among the ceratioid anglerfishes) *jordani* (for David Starr Jordan, possibly America's greatest ichthyologist).

MELANOCETIDAE (BLACKDEVIL FAMILY)
Common Blackdevil
Melanocetus johnsonii Günther

Distinguishing characters. — This small black anglerfish has a short fishing pole, a terminal bait, and more than 11 dorsal rays. The well-developed underslung lower jaw, moderate-sized upper jaw, dentition, relatively large head, and enormous gape of the mouth are characteristic of the common blackdevil. Typically the body is strongy pigmented and moderately flabby, and the skin is smooth.

Natural history notes. — *Melanocetus johnsonii* is known from all oceans. Many specimens have been obtained during oceanic trawling operations and deepsea investigations. The largest known individual (a female) is about 5 inches long.

[127]

Small larvae, less than an eighth of an inch long, lack pigment, but at about that size the dorsal surface of the tail region (caudal peduncle) becomes pigmented. This color pattern in larvae remains constant up to metamorphosis.

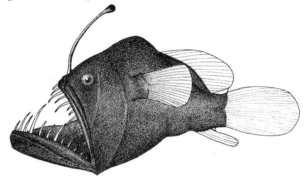

Fig. 70. *Melanocetus johnsonii*

Females are darkly pigmented after metamorphosis, except for their fins and fishing pole. The fins and illicium do not become pigmented until the fish reaches a length of about 2 inches. During this early period the jaw teeth lengthen and become well-developed fangs.

Males are poorly known. The largest male larva measures 17 millimeters (about two-thirds of an inch) and is similar to females of the same size and shape. At metamorphosis, males become more slender, the gelatinous layer around the body is reduced, and the naked skin turns a light brown. Males of this family are free-living and toothless.

Fishery information. — All known blackdevils have been captured in midwater trawls, plankton nets, and other collecting gear during exploratory fishing operations by scientific personnel. Successful operations have yielded specimens from near the surface and as deep as 7,500 feet.

Other family members. — This family is represented by a single genus, *Melanocetus.* Eight species are included in the genus, with only one known from off California. Seven species, including *M. johnsonii,* are known from the Pacific Ocean. None of the other species has been taken closer to California than the Gulf of Panama.

Meaning of name. — *Melanocetus* (in reference to any large black sea animal; here the meaning is probably blackwhale) *johnsonii* (named for a Mr. Johnson of Madeira who found the first individual).

CERATIIDAE (SEADEVIL FAMILY)
Triplewart Seadevil
Cryptopsarus couesii Gill

Distinguishing characters. — This elongate whale-shaped anglerfish has a short fishing pole and lure. Diagnostic of seadevils are the three globular, gland-like modified dorsal rays sunk in the skin just anterior to the dorsal fin. In addition to these caruncles, triple-wart seadevils have few dorsal rays (4 to 5) and few

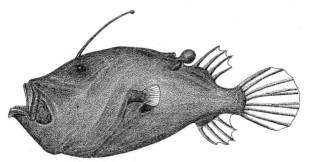

Fig. 71. *Cryptopsarus couesii*

anal fin rays (4). The skin is beset with tiny spines, and small pectoral fins originate midway up the side of the body. The mouth is slightly superior (high up), and the bait on the fishing pole is globular.

[129]

The modified caudal fins of seadevils differ from those of all other anglerfishes. The two central (innermost) rays of the tail fin are longest, the four innermost rays are branched and prolonged, and all rays have club-shaped thickenings at their tips. These thickenings, which have somewhat the appearance of the caruncles, may function as light-producing glands.

Natural history notes. — Cryptopsarus couesii has been taken from all oceans, but it was first recorded for the California fauna from a specimen taken in Monterey Bay. The largest known seadevil (not from our waters) was a female measuring 440 millimeters (about 18 inches.)

Larvae develop the globular caruncles typical of the family when about one-fifth of an inch long. These typical ceratiid larvae are distinguished by their round globular shape, the low number of rays in their unpaired fins, caruncles, and a peculiar scarflike band of pigment around the head.

Males are free-living as adolescents but parasitic as adults. These small anglerfishes are naked, spineless, lack caruncles, lack pigment typical of the females, and are toothless. However, larval teeth are present in the adolescents. At metamorphosis the head and body stretch out, decreasing the body dimensions relative to the total length.

Females have dark brown or black skin impregnated with small close-set pointed spines. The mouth is moderately large, measuring about half of the total length. After metamorphosis the caruncles grow at a differential rate, so their size for any given female is highly variable.

Fishery information. — All ceratiids have been taken with deep-sea fishing gear operated by scientific personnel. Successful trawls have yielded seadevils from surface operations and from depths as great as 5,000 feet.

Other family members. — Only two genera are allocated to this family, *Cryptopsarus* and *Ceratias*, each containing but a single species. Only *Cryptopsarus couesii* occurs off California.

Meaning of name. — *Cryptopsarus* (a hidden or concealed *Sarus*, or lizard-like fish) *couesii* (named for the eminent ornithologist Elliot Coues).

LINOPHRYNIDAE (NETDEVIL FAMILY)
Blacktail Netdevil
Linophryne coronata Parr

Distinguishing characters. — The blacktail netdevil, a small anglerfish, has a moderately elongated fishing pole (illicium), a long barbel originating near the tip of the lower jaw, and a fat, globular black body. Furthermore, the lower half of each jaw fang is black. The central part of the caudal fin lacks pigment, but is bordered on its other edges by a narrow black band.

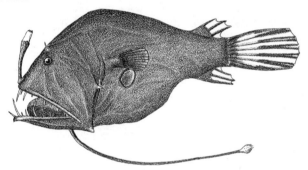

Fig. 72. *Linophryne coronata*

Natural history notes. — Only a single specimen of *Linophryne coronata* is known from off southern California, although members of the family are known from all the oceans of the world. The largest known female is 100 millimeters (4 inches) long.

Juveniles have longer sphenotic spines on the top

of the head, longer teeth, and longer fishing lures and baits than adults. Larvae typically are slender, but body depth increases with age.

The free-living adolescent males are black or brownish, teeth are usually absent, eyes are usually small, and the body is slender. After metamorphosis the small males seek out females and become parasitic. No males were noted on the single female from off California. In all young netdevils the anal opening is displaced from the ventral body midline to the left side of the belly.

Females have smooth skin, a large broad head on a short body, and, in certain members of the family, somewhat "telescopic" eyes.

Fishery information. — The only captures that we could verify were made with midwater trawling gear, usually at moderate depths — 2,000 feet and deeper.

Other family members. — Five genera are currently recognized in the netdevil family, but only *Linophryne* is known from off California. The other four genera are known from the Pacific Ocean, but none has been recorded closer than the Gulf of Panama and the south Pacific. Current classification indicates that there are fifteen species of *Linophryne,* and seven of these occur in the Pacific Ocean, but only *L. coronata* is known from within 1,000 miles of California.

Meaning of name. — *Linophryne* (toad that fishes with a net) *coronata* (in reference to a crown or wreath).

ONEIRODIDAE (DREAMER FAMILY)
Pacific Dreamer
Oneirodes acanthias (Gilbert)

Distinguishing characters. — The Pacific dreamer is a moderate-sized black anglerfish with a fishing pole one-fifth of its total length. Features which will aid in identification are the long equal-sized jaws filled with well-developed sharp teeth, a large gaping mouth extending beyond the eye, a fishing pole originating on the snout, and a lack of black skin on the caudal fin. Loose smooth skin covers the body like a sack dress. A number of spines on the head, above the eyes, and behind the jaws are well formed and sharp in this species. Larvae are distinguished by their oblong bodies, pigment patterns, inflated skin, and lack of ventral fins.

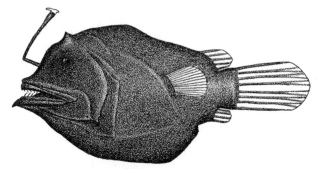

Fig. 73. *Oneirodes acanthias*

Natural history notes. — *Oneirodes acanthias* is found only in the eastern north Pacific between the Gulf of Alaska and the vicinity of Cedros Island, Baja California (at least). It is the most abundant member of its family off California. Pacific dreamers live at depths considerably greater than 1,000 feet; they do not undertake diurnal, vertical migrations. More than fifty adult females have been captured off southern California, ranging in length from 1 to 8 inches. The largest Pacific dreamer we know of, which is probably not full grown, weighs less than eight ounces. The otoliths of a 5-inch female contained seven winter rings, so Pacific dreamers are probably older than ten years at maximum size.

Although adult females are commonly taken off California, few young individuals have been collected. In other oneirodids, more larvae than metamorphosed specimens are known. Young dreamers differ from most other anglerfishes in that they attain adult form even when quite small. Males of *O. acanthias* are free-living, lack teeth, and have their eyes directed outward rather than up. They have much larger heads than either larvae or females. Metamorphosed females develop an isolated ray on the back between the eyes and dorsal fin. This ray is a vestigial part of the fishing-pole mechanism, and is typical of all members of the genus *Oneirodes*. Most members of the family feed heavily on crustaceans, although they are well equipped to feed on other deep-sea forms.

Fishery information. — In the eastern north Pacific, *O. acanthias* has been captured only with midwater trawling gear in deep water. Postmetamorphosed juveniles are occasionally taken near shore in "shallow basins" but never above 1,000 feet. Larvae are known to occur in the upper 1,000 feet, but are seldom caught with midwater trawls.

Other family members. — The dreamer family has fifteen variously specialized genera which possess few features in common to distinguish them, as a group, from other anglerfishes. Five oneirodids occur off California: *Chaenophryne, Dolopichthys, Lophodolus, Microlophichthys,* and *Oneirodes. Chaenophryne* lacks spines on the head and has a smooth round body. The illicium of *Lophodolus* arises from between the spines on top of the head rather than on the snout. *Dolopichthys* and *Microlophichthys* resemble *Oneirodes* in that the fishing pole originates on the snout, but both have black skin on the tail. *Microlophichthys* has a very short fishing pole with a bait (esca) that is more than half the total length of the pole; in *Dolopichthys* the lure is much shorter than the fishing pole itself. Nine species of *Oneirodes* are recognized, but only two occur off California. *Oneirodes eschrichtii* differs from *acanthias* in the shape and ornamentation of the lure on the fishing pole.

Meaning of name. — *Oneirodes* (something out of a dream, in reference to its almost unbelievable shape) *acanthias* (a prickly thing, pertaining to the spines on the head).

GIGANTACTINIDAE (WHIPNOSE FAMILY)
Longpole Whipnose
Gigantactis macronema Regan

Distinguishing characters. — This black anglerfish is immediately recognizable by its enormously elongated fishing pole (illicium). The illicium may be four times the body length. Other characteristics serving to distinguish whipnoses are the spinulose skin, slender and firm body, moderately strong teeth in juveniles and adults, and very small eyes.

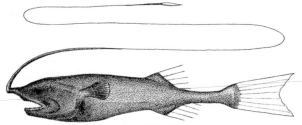

Fig. 74. *Gigantactis macronema*

Natural history notes. — Six of the seven known individuals of *Gigantactis macronema* have been captured off California. The other individual is the type from the northwest Atlantic Ocean. These rare deep-sea fishes are seldom taken except by specialized fishery gear. Although less than thirty metamorphosed whipnose anglerfishes (all species) are known, they are distributed over all the oceans. The largest known female of *Gigantactis* (not *G. macronema*) measures just under 24 inches. The otoliths of a 6-inch specimen of *G. macronema* had three winter rings; the fish did not appear to have attained maturity at this size and age, however. A 2-foot relative captured near

San Clemente Island was over eighteen years old judged by the rings on its otoliths.

Whipnose larvae differ from adults in having a short body and very inflated skin. Gigantactinid young are similar to caulophrynid larvae in having very large pectoral fins reaching to or beyond the tail, but young whipnoses lack ventral fins and thus are readily recognized. Several kinds of gigantactinid larvae can be distinguished by dorsal and peritoneal pigment, and by the numbers of dorsal and anal fin rays. Several hundred whipnose larvae have been collected but not identified.

Females become densely pigmented after metamorphosis, but the skin remains inflated for a short period. Upon metamorphosis the pectoral fins decrease in size, the illicium grows rapidly, the lateral line organs on the head develop into filaments, and the individual takes on the adult appearance. These changes occur before the females are 2 inches long.

Metamorphosed free-living males are as rare in collections as females, only ten being known. These are characterized by slender bodies, small pectoral fins, dark skin, denticles in jaws rather than teeth, and greatly enlarged nostrils.

Whipnose anglerfishes seem to be active predators, feeding on other midwater fishes, including *Cyclothone acclinidens, Triphoturus mexicanus,* and *Bathylagus stilbius;* cephalopods, including *Vampyroteuthis;* and miscellaneous invertebrates such as amphipods, natant decapod crustaceans, and several kinds of coelenterates.

Fishery information. — Almost all whipnoses have been collected during oceanic exploratory fishing aboard research vessels. Individuals have been taken near the surface and to a depth of 5,000 feet. One large female, collected during commercial fishing off Florida, was retained by the fisherman, which is unfortunate when a rare species is involved.

Other family members. — The family is represented by two genera, *Gigantactis* and *Rhynchactis*. Of the ten described species of *Gigantactis*, only one occurs off California, although an undescribed form has recently been taken in deep water off southern California. The monotypic genus *Rhynchactis* has not been taken from waters within the state boundaries.

Meaning of name. — *Gigantactis* (in reference to a giant touching structure, the fishing pole) *macronema* (long thread, in reference to the longest fishing pole).

APPENDIX I

CHECKLIST OF DEEP-WATER TELEOSTEAN FISHES FROM OFF CALIFORNIA

Alepocephalidae
Alepocephalus tenebrosus Gilbert, 1891
Bajacalifornia burragei Townsend & Nichols, 1925
Brunichthys asperifrons (Garman, 1899)
Ericara salmoneum Gill & Townsend, 1897
Narcetes stomias (Gilbert, 1890)
Photostylus pycnopterus Beebe, 1933
Talismania bifurcata (Parr, 1951)

Searsiidae
Holtbyrnia macrops Maul, 1957
Holtbyrnia melanocephala (Vaillant, 1888)
Maulisia mauli Parr, 1960
Mirorictus taningi Parr, 1947
Normichthys campbelli Lavenberg, 1965
Pellisolus facilis Parr, 1951
Sagamichthys abei Parr, 1953

Argentinidae
Argentina sialis Gilbert, 1890
Microstoma microstoma (Risso, 1810)
Nansenia candida Cohen, 1958
Nansenia crassa Lavenberg, 1965

Bathylagidae
Pathylagus milleri Jordan & Gilbert, 1898
Bathylagus nigrigenys Parr, 1931
Bathylagus ochotensis Schmidt, 1938
Bathylagus pacificus Gilbert, 1890
Bathylagus stilbius (Gilbert, 1890)
Bathylagus wesethi Bolin, 1939

Opisthoproctidae
Bathylychnops exilis Cohen, 1958
Dolichopteryx brachyrhynchus Parr, 1937
Dolichopteryx longipes (Vaillant, 1888)
Macropinna microstoma Chapman, 1939
Opisthoproctus soleatus Vaillant, 1888

Gonostomatidae
Cyclothone acclinidens Garman, 1899
Cyclothone alba Brauer, 1906
Cyclothone atraria Gilbert, 1905

Cyclothone braueri Jespersen & Tåning, 1926
Cyclothone pallida Brauer, 1902
Cyclothone pseudopallida Mukhacheva, 1964
Cyclothone signata Garman, 1899
Danaphos oculatus (Garman, 1899)
Gonostoma atlanticum Norman, 1930
Ichthyococcus elongatus Imai, 1941
Ichthyococcus irregularis Rechnitzer & Böhlke, 1958.
Valenciennellus stellatus Garman, 1899
Vinciguerria lucetia (Garman, 1899)
Vinciguerria nimbaria (Jordan & Williams, 1895)
Vinciguerria poweriae (Cocco, 1838)
Woodsia nonsuchae (Beebe, 1932)
Sternoptychidae
Argyropelecus hawaiensis Schultz, 1960
Argyropelecus intermedius Clarke, 1877
Argyropelecus lychnus Garman, 1899
Argyropelecus pacificus Schultz, 1960
Sternoptyx diaphana Hermann, 1781
Stomiatidae
Stomias atriventer Garman, 1899
Melanostomiatidae
Bathophilus brevis Regan & Trewavas, 1930
Bathophilus flemingi Aron & McCrery, 1958
Flagellostomias boureei (Zugmayer, 1913)
Melanostomias valdiviae Brauer, 1902
Opostomias mitsuii Imai, 1941
Photonectes margarita (Goode & Bean, 1896)
Tactostoma macropus Bolin, 1939
Malacosteidae
Aristostomias scintillans (Gilbert, 1915)
Idiacanthidae
Idiacanthus antrostomus Gilbert, 1890
Chauliodontidae
Chauliodus macouni Bean, 1890
Astronesthidae
Borostomias panamensis Regan & Trewavas, 1930
Neonesthes capensis (Gilchrist & von Bonde, 1924)
Bathylaconidae
Bathylaco nigricans Goode & Bean, 1896
Giganturidae
Bathyleptus lisae Walters, 1961
Neoscopelidae
Scopelengys tristis Alcock, 1892
Myctophidae
Centrobranchus chaerocephalus Fowler, 1903

Ceratoscopelus townsendi (Eigenmann & Eigenmann, 1889)
Diaphus andersoni Tåning, 1932
Diaphus glandulifera Gilbert, 1913
Diaphus protoculus (Gilbert, 1890)
Diaphus theta Eigenmann & Eigenmann, 1890
Diogenichthys atlanticus (Taning, 1928)
Diogenichthys laternatus (Garman, 1899)
Electrona rissoi (Cocco, 1829)
Gonichthys tenuiculus (Garman, 1899)
Hygophum reinhardtii (Lutken, 1892)
Lampadena urophaos Paxton, 1963
Lampanyctus jordani Gilbert, 1913
Lampanyctus niger (Günther, 1887)
Lampanyctus regalis (Gilbert, 1891)
Lampanyctus ritteri Gilbert, 1915
Lampanyctus steinbecki Bolin, 1939
Lampanyctus tenuiformis (Brauer, 1906)
Lepidophanes pyrsobolus (Alcock, 1890)
Loweina rara (Lütken, 1892)
Myctophum nitidulum Garman, 1899
Notolychnus valdiviae (Brauer, 1904)
Notoscopelus resplendens Richardson, 1844
Parvilux ingens Hubbs & Wisner, 1964
Protomyctophum crockeri (Bolin, 1939)
Protomyctophum thompsoni (Chapman, 1944)
Stenobrachius leucopsarus (Eigenmann & Eigenmann, 1890)
Stenobrachius nannochir (Gilbert, 1890)
Symbolophorus californiensis (Eigenmann & Eigenmann, 1889)
Taaningichthys bathyphilus (Tåning, 1928)
Taaningichthys minimus (Tåning, 1928)
Tarletonbeania crenularis (Jordan & Gilbert, 1880)
Triphoturus mexicanus (Gilbert, 1890)
Paralepididae
Lestidium johnfitchi Rofen, 1959
Lestidium ringens (Jordan & Gilbert, 1880)
Lestidium sphyraenopsis (Hubbs, 1916)
Macroparalepis macrurus Ege, 1933
Notolepis rissoi (Bonaparte, 1841)
Paralepis atlantica Kroyer, 1891
Sudis atrox Rofen, 1963
Alepisauridae
Alepisaurus ferox Lowe, 1833
Anotopteridae
Anotopterus pharao Zugmayer, 1911

Scopelarchidae
Benthalbella dentata (Chapman, 1939)
Benthalbella infans Zugmayer, 1911
Benthalbella linguidens (Mead & Böhlke, 1953)
Scopelarchus analis Brauer, 1902
Scopelarchus nicholsi (Parr, 1929)
Scopelosauridae
Scopelosaurus harryi (Mead, 1953)
Scopelosaurus sp.
Nettastomatidae
Facciolella gilbertii (Garman, 1899)
Venefica procera (Goode & Bean, 1883)
Venefica tentaculata Garman, 1899
Congridae
Gnathophis catalinensis (Wade, 1946)
Xenomystax atrarius Gilbert, 1891
Ophichthidae (includes Myrophidae)
Hesperomyrus fryi Myers & Storey, 1939
Myrichthys tigrinus Girard, 1859
Ophichthus triserialis (Kaup, 1856)
Ophichthus zophochir Jordan & Gilbert, 1881
Derichthyidae
Derichthys serpentinus Gill, 1884
Serrivomeridae
Serrivomer sector Garman, 1899
Nemichthyidae
Avocettina gilli (Bean, 1890)
Avocettina infans (Günther, 1878)
Nemichthys scolopaceus Richardson, 1848
Cyemidae
Cyema atrum Günther, 1878
Saccopharyngidae
Saccopharynx sp.
Eurypharyngidae
Eurypharynx pelecanoides Vaillant, 1882
Cetomimidae
Cetomimus sp.
Cetostomus regani (Zugmayer, 1914)
Ditropichthys storeri (Goode & Bean, 1895)
Rondeletiidae
Rondeletia loricata Abe & Hotta, 1963
Moridae
Antimora rostrata (Günther, 1878)
Melanonus zugmayeri Norman, 1930
Physiculus rastrelliger Gilbert, 1890

[141]

Macrouridae
  Coelorhynchus scaphopsis (Gilbert, 1890)
  Coryphaenoides abyssorum (Gilbert, 1915)
  Coryphaenoides acrolepis (Bean, 1883)
  Coryphaenoides pectoralis (Gilbert, 1891)
  Nezumia liolepis (Gilbert, 1890)
  Nezumia stelgidolepis (Gilbert, 1890)
Ophidiidae
  Otophidium scrippsi Hubbs, 1916
  Otophidium taylori (Girard, 1858)
Brotulidae
  Brosmophycis marginata (Ayres, 1854)
  Cataetyx rubrirostris Gilbert, 1890
  Dicrolene sp.
  Lamprogrammus niger Alcock, 1891
  Oligopus diagrammus (Heller & Snodgrass, 1903)
Zoarcidae
  Aprodon cortezianus Gilbert, 1890
  Bothrocara brunneum (Bean, 1890)
  Bothrocara molle Bean, 1890
  Bothrocara remigerum Gilbert, 1915
  Embryx crassilabris (Gilbert, 1890)
  Embryx crotalina (Gilbert, 1890)
  Embryx parallela Gilbert, 1915
  Lycenchelys jordani (Evermann & Goldsborough, 1907)
  Lycodapus attenuatus Gilbert, 1915
  Lycodapus dermatinus Gilbert, 1895
  Lycodapus fierasfer Gilbert, 1890
  Lycodapus lycodon Gilbert, 1915
  Lycodapus mandibularis Gilbert, 1915
  Lycodes diapterus Gilbert, 1891
  Lycodopsis pacifica (Collett, 1879)
  Lyconema barbatum Gilbert, 1893
  Maynea californica Gilbert, 1915
  Melanostigma pammelas Gilbert, 1893
Macrorhamphosidae
  Macrorhamphosis gracilis (Lowe, 1839)
Oreosomatidae
  Allocyttus folletti Myers, 1960
Zeidae
  Zenopsis nebulosa (Temminck & Schlegel, 1845)
Lampridae
  Lampris regius (Bonnaterre, 1788)
Lophotidae
  Lophotus cristatus Johnson, 1863

Trachipteridae
  Desmodema polystictum (Ogilby, 1897)
  Trachipterus altivelis Kner, 1858
  Trachipterus fukuzakii Fitch, 1964
  Zu cristatus (Bonelli, 1820)
Regalecidae
  Regalecus glesne (Ascanius, 1788)
Melamphaidae
  Melamphaes acanthomus Ebeling, 1962
  Melamphaes longivelis Parr, 1933
  Melamphaes lugubris Gilbert, 1890
  Melamphaes parvus Ebeling, 1962
  Poromitra crassiceps (Günther, 1878)
  Scopeloberyx robustus (Günther, 1887)
  Scopelogadus mizolepis bispinosus (Gilbert, 1890)
Anoplogasteridae
  Anoplogaster cornuta (Valenciennes, 1829)
Cheilodipteridae
  Howella brodiei (Ogilby, 1898)
Bramidae
  Brama japonica Hilgendorf, 1878
  Pteraclis velifera (Pallas, 1770)
  Taractes longipinnis (Lowe, 1843)
Caristiidae
  Caristius macropus (Bellotti, 1903)
Pentacerotidae
  Pentaceros richardsoni Smith, 1849
Uranoscopidae
  Kathetostoma averruncus Jordan & Bollman, 1889
Chiasmodontidae
  Chiasmodon niger Johnson, 1863
  Kali normani (Parr, 1931)
  Pseudoscopelus altipinnis Parr, 1933
  Pseudoscopelus scriptus Lütken, 1892
Icosteidae
  Icosteus aenigmaticus Lockington, 1880
Trichiuridae
  Assurger anzac (Alexander, 1916)
  Lepidopus xantusi Goode & Bean, 1896
  Trichiurus nitens Garman, 1899
Gempylidae
  Gempylus serpens Cuvier, 1829
  Lepidocybium flavobrunneum (Smith, 1849)
  Ruvettus pretiosus Cocco, 1833
Luvaridae
  Luvarus imperialis Rafinesque, 1810

Tetragonuridae
  Tetragonurus cuvieri Risso, 1810
Centrolophidae
  Icichthys lockingtoni Jordan & Gilbert, 1880
Nomeidae
  Cubiceps gracilis (Lowe, 1843)
  Psenes pellucidus Lütken, 1880
Zaniolepididae
  Zaniolepis frenata Eigenmann, 1889
  Zaniolepis latipinnis Girard, 1857
Agonidae
  Agonopsis emmelane (Jordan & Starks, 1895)
  Agonopsis sterletus (Gilbert, 1896)
  Asterotheca infraspinata (Gilbert, 1904)
  Asterotheca pentacantha (Gilbert, 1890)
  Bothragonus swanii (Steindachner, 1877)
  Occa verrucosa (Lockington, 1880)
  Odontopyxis trispinosa Lockington, 1879
  Pallasina barbata aix Starks, 1896
  Stelgis vulsa (Jordan & Gilbert, 1880)
  Stellerina xyosterna (Jordan & Gilbert, 1880)
  Xeneretmus latifrons (Gilbert, 1890)
  Xeneretmus leiops Gilbert, 1915
  Xeneretmus ritteri Gilbert, 1915
  Xeneretmus triacanthus (Gilbert, 1890)
Liparididae
  Careproctus melanurus Gilbert, 1890
  Careproctus osborni (Townsend & Nichols, 1925)
  Liparis florae (Jordan & Starks, 1895)
  Liparis fucensis Gilbert, 1896
  Liparis mucosus Ayres, 1855
  Liparis pulchellus Ayres, 1855
  Liparis rutteri (Gilbert & Snyder, 1898)
  Lipariscus nanus Gilbert, 1915
  Nectoliparis pelagicus Gilbert & Burke, 1912
  Paraliparis albescens Gilbert, 1915
  Paraliparis caudatus Gilbert, 1915
  Paraliparis cephalus Gilbert, 1891
  Paraliparis dactylosus Gilbert, 1896
  Paraliparis deani Burke, 1912
  Paraliparis mento Gilbert, 1891
  Paraliparis rosaceus Gilbert, 1890
  Paraliparis ulochir Gilbert, 1896
  Rhinoliparis attenuatus Burke, 1912
  Rhinoliparis barbulifer Gilbert, 1895

Lophiidae
  Chirolophius spilurus (Garman, 1899)
Ogcocephalidae
  Zalieutes elater (Jordan & Gilbert, 1882)
Caulophrynidae
  Caulophryne jordani Goode & Bean, 1896
Melanocetidae
  Melanocetus johnsonii Günther, 1864
Ceratiidae
  Cryptopsarus couesii Gill, 1883
Linophrynidae
  Linophryne coronata Parr, 1927
Oneirodidae
  Chaenophryne parviconus Regan & Trewavas, 1932
  Dolopichthys longicornis Parr, 1927
  Lophodolus acanthognathus Regan, 1925
  Microlophichthys microlophus (Regan, 1925)
  Oneirodes acanthias (Gilbert, 1915)
  Oneirodes eschrichtii Lütken, 1871
Gigantactinidae
  Gigantactis macronema Regan, 1925

APPENDIX II

Organizations in California With Collections of Deep-Water Fishes or Engaged in Research

Although about twenty universities, governmental agencies, and museums have collections of deep-water fishes for display or research purposes or both, fewer than a third of these have major collections, or are sponsoring extensive research and collecting programs (indicated by asterisk in appropriate column). Only five of the organizations listed below have large research vessels capable of working considerable distances offshore for extensive periods: Scripps Institution of Oceanography, Naval Electronics Laboratory, U.S. Bureau of Commercial Fisheries, California Department of Fish and Game, and the University of Southern California.

Most other colleges in California, many high schools, a few other public museums and several private ones, and many individual collectors undoubtedly have a jar or two of preserved deep-sea fishes, or an assortment of fossil "imprints" and similar fragmentia, but for obvious reasons these are not listed.

Organization	Preserved Specimens	Fossils	Engaged in research and collecting
Scripps Inst. Oceanog.	worldwide*	no	yes*
Naval Electron. Lab., San Diego	no	no	diving saucer
U.S. Bur. Commercial Fisheries, La Jolla	eastern Pacific*	no	yes*
San Diego Nat. Hist. Mus.	limited display	limited display	no
Calif. Dept. Fish and Game, Terminal Is.	eastern Pacific	yes*	yes*
Cal State, Long Beach	eastern Pacific	no	no
Cabrillo Beach Mus., San Pedro	limited display	limited	no

		display	
Univ. Calif. Los Angeles	eastern Pacific	no	yes
Univ. S. Calif.	Antarctic*	no	yes*
Los Angeles County Museum	Pacific Ocean and Antarctic*	yes*	yes*
Univ. Calif., Santa Barbara	eastern Pacific	no	yes*
Santa Barbara Nat. Hist. Mus.	eastern Pacific	no	no
Cal. Poly., San Luis Obispo	eastern Pacific	yes	yes
Hopkins Marine Sta., Pacific Grove	eastern Pacific	no	yes
Aquatic Research Inst., Stockton	limited groups	no	yes
Stanford Univ. Nat. Hist. Mus.	worldwide*	yes*	yes
Cal. Acad. Sciences,, San Francisco	Pacific Ocean	yes	yes
Univ. Calif., Berkeley	eastern Pacific	no	no
Cal State, Arcata	eastern Pacific	no	no

APPENDIX III

These references provide keys and other information needed for identifying deep-sea fishes belonging to families containing too many individuals for us to differentiate satisfactorily within the limitations of this booklet. A few general works and a recently published proposed classification of teleostean fishes are included.

Bayliff, William H. 1959. Notes on the taxonomy and distribution of certain zoarcid fishes in the northeastern Pacific Copeia 1959 (1):78-80.

Bertelsen, E. 1951. The ceratioid fishes. Dana-Rept. 39:1-276.

Bolin, Rolf L. 1939. A review of the myctophid fishes of the Pacific Coast of the United States and of Lower California. Stanford Ichthyol. Bull. 1(4):89-156.

———. 1959. Iniomi, Myctophidae from the "Michael Sars" north Atlantic deep-sea expedition 1910. Rept. Michael Sars N. Atl. Deep-Sea Exped. 1910, 4(7):1-45.

Burke, Victor. 1930. Revision of the fishes of the family Liparidae. Bull. U. S. Nat. Mus. 150:1-204.

Clemens, W. A., and G. V. Wilby. 1961. Fishes of the Pacific Coast of Canada (2d ed). Bull. Fish. Res. Bd. Canada 68:1-443.

Ebeling, Alfred W. 1962. Melamphaidae. I. Systematics and zoogeography of the species in the bathypelagic fish genus *Melamphaes* Günther. Dana-Rept. 58:1-164.

Ebeling, Alfred W., and W. H. Weed III. 1963. Melamphaidae. III. Systematics and distribution of the species in the bathypelagic fish genus *Scopelogadus* Vaillant. Dana-Rept. 60:1-58.

Fitch, John E. 1966. The poacher *Asterotheca infraspinata* (Gilbert) added to California's marine fauna, and a key to Californian Agonidae (Pisces). Calif. Fish and Game 52(2): 121-124.

Fraser-Brunner, A. 1949. A classification of the fishes of the family Myctophidae. Proc. Zool. Soc. London 118(4):1019-1106.

Greenwood, P. Humphry, D. E. Rosen, S. H. Weitzman, and G. S. Myers. 1966. Phyletic studies of teleostean fishes with a provisional classification of living forms. Bull. Am. Mus. Nat. Hist. 131(4):339-456.

Grey, Marion. 1964. Family Gonostomatidae. *In* Fishes of the western north Atlantic. Sears Found. Mar. Res. Mem. 1, 1(4):78-240.

Jordan, David Starr. 1963. The genera of fishes and a classification of fishes. Reprinted with a new foreword by George S. Myers, Stanford University, and the comprehensive index by Hugh M. Smith and Leonard P. Schultz, U. S. National Museum. Stanford Univ. Press. 800 pp.

McAllister, D. E., and E. I. S. Rees. 1964. A revision of the eelpout genus *Melanostigma* with a new genus and comments on *Maynea*. Nat. Mus. Canada, Contrib. Zool. Bull. 199(5):85-110.

Mukhacheva, V. A. 1964. On the genus *Cyclothone* (Gonostomatidae, Pisces) of the Pacific Ocean. Trudy Okean. Inst., Akad. Nauk SSSR 73:93-138 [In Russian with English summary.]

Olsen, Yngve H., editor. 1964. Fishes of the western north Atlantic. Part 4. Order Isospondyli, in part (argentinoids, stomiatoids, esocoids, bathylaconoids) and Order Giganturoidei. Sears Found. Mar. Res. Mem. 1. 599 pp.

———. 1966. Fishes of the western north Atlantic. Part 5. Order Iniomi, Order Lyomeri. Sears Found. Mar. Res. Mem. 1. 647 pp.

Parr, A. E. 1960. The fishes of the family Searsidae. Dana-Rept. 51:1-109.

amphipod: group name for small shrimp-like and crab-like creatures (Amphipoda) that often are fed upon by fishes.

barbel: a slender fleshy "chin whisker" found in many kinds of fishes and which functions primarily as a sensory organ for locating food.

bathypelagic: a somewhat arbitrary depth zone in offshore or oceanic waters, usually below 3,000 feet and above 10,000.

branchiostegal rays: bones in a fish's throat region, usually elongate, connected by a membrane, and folded like a fan beneath the opercles.

caruncle: a globular, glandlike modified dorsal finray found in the anglerfish *Cryptopsarus.*

caudal peduncle: the tapered, posterior fleshy part of a fish just in front of the tail fin.

cephalopod: group name for squids and octopuses.

cirrus: a filament or slender fleshy appendage usually found in the head region.

coelenterate: group name for jellyfishes, medusae and similar closely related gelatinous animals.

ctenoid scale: a scale with a rough, comb-like or toothed margin.

ctenophore: group name for gelatinous marine invertebrates having oval or band-shaped bodies and eight meridional rows of ciliated plates.

cycloid scale: a smooth edged more or less circular scale with concentric striations.

diatomite: a fine siliceous earth composed mainly of cell walls of one-celled marine algae (diatoms).

esca: the "bait" or lure at the tip of the illicium or angling device sported by many anglerfishes.

euphausiids: group name for krill or shrimp-like creatures that abound in much of the marine environment.

faunal zone: a region or area that because of temperature, salinity, food, shelter and other factors is suited for certain definite associations of animals.

frontal ridges: bony ridges on the frontal bones (above the eyes) of some fishes.

hermaphrodite: an animal having both male and female organs.

humeral spine: a spine in the shoulder region as occurs on the anglerfish *Chirolophius*.

illicium: the first two dorsal finrays modified into a fishing pole in some anglerfishes.

leptocephalus: a transparent elongate or leaf-shaped larval stage that occurs in some fishes, especially eels.

mesopelagic: a somewhat arbitrary depth zone in offshore or oceanic waters, usually below 600 feet and above 3,000.

metamorphosis: a change of form or transformation such as occurs among eels between the larval and adult stages.

mysid: group name for shrimp-like creatures that abound in the world oceans.

otolith: a calcareous concretion in the inner ear of a fish, functioning as an organ of hearing and balance in the fish, and used by biologists for determining fish ages, identification, and other data.

pectoral fins: paired fins that usually originate near mid-side immediately posterior to the gill opening.

pelvic fins: paired fins that usually originate on the ventral side of the fish in front of the anal opening, sometimes also referred to as ventral fins.

photophore: a complicated organ for emitting light or luminescing, highly developed among lanternfishes, gonostomatids, and numerous other families of deep-sea fishes.

polychaete: group name for segmented marine worms that have swimming appendages with many chaetae or bristles.

pseudobranchia: tiny gill-like structures (false gills) found under the upper part of the gill cover in most bony fishes about on a level with the fish's eye.

purse-seine: a net that is used to surround schools of fish and which is then closed at the bottom (pursed) to trap the encircled fish.

pyrosome: group name for pelagic colonial animals that resemble somewhat a gelatinous tube, shaped like the finger of a glove. Pyrosomes are luminous at night.

scattering layer: any concentration of living organisms (fish, crustaceans, cephalopods, medusae, and others) that forms a layer at any depth beneath the sea surface and above the bottom; signals transmitted by sonar are reflected back to the surface from organisms in a scattering layer.

sexual dimorphism: a phenomenon in which males and females differ markedly in shape, size, color, or other ways.

sphenotic spine: spines that originate on the sphenotic bone above and slightly behind the eye.

taxonomy: the science of classification at all levels starting with the individual and arranging or grouping according to relationships.

trawl net: a sac-like net that is towed through the water to capture fish. Otter trawls and beam trawls are usually dragged along the floor of the sea, while midwater trawls are fished at any depth beneath the surface.

INDEX